Noble Truths, Noble Path

THE TEACHINGS OF THE BUDDHA SERIES

The Connected Discourses of the Buddha:
A Translation of the Saṃyutta Nikāya

Great Disciples of the Buddha:
Their Lives, Their Works, Their Legacy

In the Buddha's Words:
An Anthology of Discourses from the Pāli Canon

The Long Discourses of the Buddha:
A Translation of the Dīgha Nikāya

The Middle Length Discourses of the Buddha:
A Translation of the Majjhima Nikāya

The Suttanipāta:
An Ancient Collection of the Buddha's Discourses
Together with Its Commentaries

The Numerical Discourses of the Buddha:
A Translation of the Aṅguttara Nikāya

The Buddha's Teachings on Social and Communal Harmony

THE TEACHINGS OF THE BUDDHA

Noble Truths, Noble Path

The Heart Essence *of the* Buddha's Original Teachings

Texts compiled, introduced, and translated

by

Bhikkhu Bodhi

Wisdom

The publisher would like to acknowledge the kind contribution made toward the printing of this book from Wong Tak Wai, Yip Pui Pui Patti Wong, Wynne Yue Tung Wong, Steve Tsang Tat Chung, Jayden Tsang, Jasper Tsang, Kathleen Wong, Ginger, Lui Wong Po Lin, Lee Chin Hung, Candy Chi, William Chi, and Meagan Chi.

Wisdom Publications
132 Perry Street
New York, NY 10014 USA
wisdomexperience.org

Library of Congress Cataloging-in-Publication Data for the hardcover edition:
Names: Bodhi, Bhikkhu, translator.
Title: Noble truths, noble path: the heart essence of the Buddha's original teachings / texts compiled, introduced, and translated by Bhikkhu Bodhi.
Description: First edition. | Somerville: Wisdom Publications, 2023. |
Series: The teachings of the Buddha | Includes bibliographical references.
Identifiers: LCCN 2022029970 (print) | LCCN 2022029971 (ebook) |
ISBN 9781614297987 (hardcover) | ISBN 9781614298243 (ebook)
Subjects: LCSH: Four Noble Truths. | Buddhism—Doctrines.
Classification: LCC BQ4230 .N63 2023 (print) | LCC BQ4230 (ebook) |
DDC 294.3/42—dc23/eng/20220818
LC record available at https://lccn.loc.gov/2022029970
LC ebook record available at https://lccn.loc.gov/2022029971

ISBN 978-1-61429-918-9 ebook ISBN 978-1-61429-824-3

28 27 26 25 24
5 4 3 2 1

Cover and interior design by Gopa & Ted 2.
Interior typesetting by PerfecType, Nashville, TN.

Printed on acid-free paper that meets the guidelines for permanence and durability of the Production Guidelines for Book Longevity of the Council on Library Resources.

Printed in Canada.

Publisher's Acknowledgment

The publisher gratefully acknowledges the generous help of the Hershey Family Foundation in sponsoring the production of this book.

Contents

Abbreviations

AN	Aṅguttara Nikāya
DN	Dīgha Nikāya
MN	Majjhima Nikāya
PTS	Pali Text Society
SN	Saṃyutta Nikāya
Sn	Suttanipāta
Spk	Sāratthappakāsinī (commentary to SN)
Sv	Sumaṅgalavilāsinī (commentary to DN)
Vibh	Vibhaṅga
Vin	Vinaya Piṭaka
Vism	Visuddhimagga

The Pāli Alphabet

The Pāli alphabet consists of 42 letters divided into 8 vowels, 33 consonants, and a nasal sound called *niggahīta*.

The 8 vowels are: *a, ā, i, ī, u, ū, e, o*.

The consonants are divided into the following groups:

Gutturals	*k*	*kh*	*g*	*gh*	*ṅ*
Palatals	*c*	*ch*	*j*	*jh*	*ñ*
Cerebrals	*ṭ*	*ṭh*	*ḍ*	*ḍh*	*ṇ*
Dentals	*t*	*th*	*d*	*dh*	*n*
Labials	*p*	*ph*	*b*	*bh*	*m*

Liquid consonants:	*r, l, ḷ, ḷh*
Semivowels:	*y, v*
Sibilant:	*s*
Aspirate:	*h*
Niggahīta:	*ṃ*

Pāli is pronounced somewhat differently in the different Theravāda countries. I describe here the Sri Lankan pronunciation, which likely corresponds more closely to the original North Indian pronunciation than that used in the Southeast Asian countries.

a as in "cut"
ā as in "ah"
i as in "king"
ī as in "keen"
u as in "put"
ū as in "pool"

e as in "ate," but before a double consonant more as in "bed"
o as in "home," but before a double consonant pronounced more briskly, as in "goat"

Of the vowels, *a, i,* and *u* are short; *ā, ī,* and *ū* are long, held twice the length of the short vowels. The vowels *e* and *o* are of variable length. They are long when they occur at the end of a syllable, as in *tesaṃ,* "to them," and *loko,* "world"; they are short when they are followed by a consonant with which they form a syllable, as in *mettā,* "loving-kindness," and *gotta,* "clan." An *o* and an *e* always carry a stress; otherwise the stress falls on a long vowel—*ā, ī, ū,* or on a double consonant, or on an internal *ṃ.*

Among the consonants, the gutturals are articulated in the throat, the palatals with the tongue against the palate. The guttural *g* is always pronounced as in "good," the palatal *c* like the *ch* in "church," the nasal *ñ* usually like the *ny* in "canyon," but before a palatal consonant (such as *c* or *j,* as in *sañjāti*) like an ordinary *n* but with the tongue against the palate. The cerebrals (also called retroflexes or linguals) are spoken with the tongue curled back, the dentals with the tongue against the upper teeth. The aspirates—*kh, gh, ch, jh, ṭh, ḍh, th, dh, ph, bh*—are single consonants each represented in Asian scripts by a single letter; they are pronounced with slightly more force than the non-aspirates. Thus *th* is pronounced as in "Thomas" (not as in "thin"); *ph* as in "puff" (not as in "phone"). Double consonants are always enunciated separately, for instance *dd* as in "mad dog," *gg* as in "big gun."

In Sri Lanka and other Theravāda Buddhist countries, the *niggahīta* is currently pronounced like *ng* in "sing," and in India like the *m* in "hum," but historically it may have been pronounced as a pure nasal vowel as in French *enfant*. It sometimes occurs inside words (for instance, in *vaṃsa,* "lineage," and *paṃsu,* "dust"); but most often it comes at the end of words following the vowels *a, i,* and *u,* for instance in *rūpaṃ, sambodhiṃ,* and *avocuṃ.*

Detailed Contents

Introduction

A couple of years ago I published a book titled *Reading the Buddha's Discourses in Pāli*, intended to help students of Buddhism learn to read the texts of the Pāli Canon in the language in which they have been preserved, the ancient Indian language now known as Pāli. The book, based on a weekly program in Pāli that I conducted over the course of three years, was primarily a Pāli-English reader, furnished with detailed grammatical explanations and a glossary. After the book was published, several of my students suggested that I prepare an anthology composed of the suttas used in that book but stripped of the linguistic and grammatical apparatus.

The present work is my response to that request. It contains all the suttas from *Reading the Buddha's Discourses*, but with the original translations slightly revised to make them more "reader friendly." In several cases I have restored portions of the original texts not included in the reader because they were less relevant to its purposes. The introductions to each chapter have been expanded to provide more background information on the material, and I have added the verses attached to a number of suttas that were not included in the reader. In chapter 4, I replaced the first sutta (SN 12:1), a concise statement of the formula of dependent origination, with the sutta that immediately follows it (SN 12:2), which amplifies the bare formula with definitions of the twelve factors. And at the end of the section on the noble eightfold path, I have added the *Oghavagga*, the "chapter on the floods," to provide a comprehensive overview of the governing purpose of the Buddhist path.

The present anthology differs significantly from another anthology I published in 2005 called *In the Buddha's Words*. The purpose of the earlier anthology was to provide a comprehensive picture of the Buddha's teaching that incorporates a wide variety of suttas into an organic structure designed to bring to light the intentional pattern underlying the Buddha's formulation of the Dhamma and thus to equip the reader with guidelines for understanding the teachings in the suttas as a whole. The structure governing that book was based on a scheme of three aims underlying the Buddha's teachings, each largely determined by the audience he was addressing and the circumstances that occasioned the discourse. These three aims are: well-being and happiness visible in this present life; well-being and happiness in future lives; and the supreme good, the attainment of nibbāna. The expression "welfare and happiness visible in this present life" refers to the happiness that comes from following ethical norms in one's family relationships, livelihood, and communal engagements. The "welfare and happiness pertaining to a future life" refers to the achievement of a fortunate rebirth, a pursuit that rests on the planks of kamma and rebirth. The third benefit the Buddha's teaching is designed to bring, the supreme or ultimate good (*paramattha*), is liberation from the cycle of repeated birth and death. This is to be achieved by cultivating the threefold higher training in moral conduct, concentration, and wisdom.

The present anthology serves a different purpose. It aims to take us straight to the heart of the Buddha's teaching, summed up in two interrelated structures: the four noble truths and the noble eightfold path. The first covers the side of doctrine, the second the side of training. These two structures are often joined together into what is called the *dhamma-vinaya*. In this compound, *dhamma* represents the teaching that illuminates the nature of things; the primary response it elicits is understanding. Its counterpart, *vinaya,* often signifies monastic discipline but can be interpreted more broadly as comprising all the factors that lead to the removal (another meaning of *vinaya*) of the mind's hindrances and fetters. The primary response it calls for is practice.

The internal unity of the Dhamma is guaranteed by the fact that the last of the four noble truths, the truth of the way, is the noble eightfold path, while the first factor of the noble eightfold path, right view, is the understanding of the four noble truths.

From this, we can see that these two mainstays of the teaching penetrate and include one another, the formula of the four noble truths containing the eightfold path and the noble eightfold path containing the four truths. Both the truths and the path are called "noble" (*ariya*). The truths are called noble because they are the truths taught by the supreme noble one, the Buddha; because they are the truths seen by the noble disciples who have arrived at the core of the Dhamma; and because they are the truths accepted as a framework of understanding by those who aspire to the status of spiritual nobility. The path is called noble because it is the path walked by all the noble ones of the past who have attained the goal and by those of the present and future who seek the fruit of clear knowledge and liberation.

The Sutta Piṭaka

The suttas or "discourses" compiled in this anthology are all taken from the Pāli Canon, the collection of texts recognized as authoritative by the Theravāda school of Buddhism, the Buddhist tradition that today flourishes in Sri Lanka and the Buddhist countries of Southeast Asia, with branches extending elsewhere throughout the world. The Pāli Canon consists of three major divisions, for which reason it is also called the Tipiṭaka, the "Three Baskets." The first is the Vinaya Piṭaka, the Basket of Monastic Discipline; the second is the Sutta Piṭaka, the Basket of Discourses, the teachings spoken by the Buddha and his leading disciples; and the third is the Abhidhamma Piṭaka, the Basket of Treatises, a rigorous systematic presentation constructed from the teachings of the Sutta Piṭaka.

While the Pāli Canon belongs to one particular Buddhist school, the texts preserved in the Sutta Piṭaka, particularly the first four collections, are not unique to the Theravāda tradition but often have parallels in the collections of other early Buddhist schools. Although these schools perished long ago, they have left behind texts still found in translations into Chinese, Tibetan, and other ancient languages; in some cases versions in Indian languages like Buddhist Hybrid Sanskrit and Gāndhārī have been found. These versions usually correspond fairly closely to their Pāli counterparts, pointing back to a common origin before the different schools went their separate ways. It is presumptuous to claim that one version of the discourses is intrinsically more archaic than the others, but since the Pāli Nikāyas are the most accessible version and are preserved in an Indian language close to the language in which they were first compiled, for practical purposes they can be regarded as the most ancient records of the Buddha's teachings available to us. They stem from the earliest period of Buddhist literary history, a period lasting roughly 150 years after the Buddha's death, and thus take us as close as possible to what the Buddha actually taught.[1]

The Sutta Piṭaka consists of five collections called Nikāyas. The four major Nikāyas are:

1. The Dīgha Nikāya: the Collection of Long Discourses, thirty-four suttas arranged into three *vaggas,* or books.
2. The Majjhima Nikāya: the Collection of Middle Length Discourses, 152 suttas arranged into three *vaggas.*
3. The Saṃyutta Nikāya: the Collection of Connected Discourses, close to three thousand short suttas grouped into fifty-six chapters, called *saṃyuttas,* which are in turn collected into five *vaggas.*
4. The Aṅguttara Nikāya: the Collection of Numerical Discourses, approximately 2,400 short suttas arranged into eleven chapters, called *nipātas.*

The Dīgha Nikāya and Majjhima Nikāya, at first glance, seem to be established principally on the basis of length: the longer discourses go into the Dīgha, the middle-length discourses into the Majjhima. But the two also appear to differ in their aims. The suttas of the Dīgha Nikāya seem to be largely directed at a popular audience, intended to inspire faith and devotion among adherents of Buddhism and to attract potential converts by demonstrating the superiority of the Buddha and his doctrine over his contemporaries. The Majjhima Nikāya seems largely directed inward toward the Buddhist community, intended to acquaint new disciples, particularly monastics, with the doctrines and practices of the Dhamma.

The Saṃyutta Nikāya is organized by way of subject matter. Each subject is the "yoke" (*saṃyoga*) that connects the discourses into a *saṃyutta* or chapter, of which there are altogether fifty-six. Hence the title of the collection, the "connected (*saṃyutta*) discourses." Since this collection provides detailed treatment of the major doctrines of Early Buddhism, it may have been intended largely for doctrinal specialists. And since many of these suttas are concerned with subjects of contemplation designed to generate direct insight into the teachings, they may also have been intended for accomplished meditators.

The Aṅguttara Nikāya is arranged according to a numerical scheme derived from a peculiar feature of the Buddha's pedagogic method. The Buddha often formulated his discourses by way of numerical sets, a format that helped to ensure that the ideas he conveyed would be easily retained in mind. The Aṅguttara Nikāya assembles these numerical discourses into a single massive work of eleven *nipātas* or chapters, each representing the number of terms upon which the constituent suttas have been framed. Such an arrangement made it especially useful for elder monastics charged with teaching junior recruits, and also for preachers in teaching the laity.

Besides the four major collections, the Sutta Piṭaka includes a fifth collection called the Khuddaka Nikāya, a name that means the Minor Collection. Originally it may have consisted merely of a number of minor works that could not be included in the four major Nikāyas. But as more and more works were added to it over the centuries, its dimensions swelled until it became the most voluminous of the five Nikāyas.

The Present Work

The suttas in this anthology have all been taken from the Saṃyutta Nikāya. I originally chose the Saṃyutta as the basis for my Pāli reader to ensure that the suttas to be studied from a linguistic angle display the fairly uniform terminology and highly structured mode of presentation typical of that collection. But there was another reason I chose the Saṃyutta as the basis for the course and for this book, a reason that pertains to the doctrinal rather than the linguistic side of the Buddhist canon. It seems that the major chapters of the Saṃyutta Nikāya, if rearranged, provide a systematic overview of the Dhamma that mirrors the pattern of the four noble truths. An anthology from this collection can thus enable the student of Early

Buddhism to see into the heart of the Buddha's teachings as directly and clearly as possible.

Before I sketch the underlying plan of this book, I should state as a precaution against misunderstanding that the texts included in this anthology are not intended to span the full range of the Buddha's teaching. They do not deal with such fundamental matters as the multiple planes of existence, the operation of kamma and its fruits, the prospects for temporal happiness, and the corresponding practices of generosity, ethical conduct, and related virtues that contribute to gradual progress toward the final goal. Rather, in relation to the three aims of the Dhamma mentioned above—well-being and happiness visible in this present life, well-being and happiness in future lives, and the ultimate good—these texts all pertain to the ultimate good, the attainment of nibbāna or liberation. They illuminate the Buddha's radical diagnosis of the human condition—and more broadly, the condition of all sentient existence—in the light of the four noble truths. They underscore the pervasive flaws inherent in the round of rebirths, trace our existential predicament to its deepest roots, and lay out the path to unraveling our bondage and winning irreversible release.

The pattern that lies at the heart of the liberating Dhamma emerges from the order of the chapters found here. The first chapter contains selections from the Saccasaṃyutta (SN 56), the Connected Discourses on the Truths—the four noble truths, which are described as "the special Dhamma teaching of the buddhas" (*buddhānaṃ sāmukkaṃsikā dhammadesanā*, for instance at DN I 110). The four noble truths serve as the most concise statement of the Dhamma, a "matrix" that generates all the other teachings and a framework into which most of those teachings can fit.

The suttas in the Saccasaṃyutta, however, seldom elaborate upon the content of the four noble truths. The *Dhammacakkappavattana Sutta* (SN 56:11), commonly known as the First Sermon, provides concise definitions of the four truths, and these are repeated in several other suttas of this *saṃyutta*. But for the most part the discourses of the Saccasaṃyutta highlight the contextual role of the four noble truths, stressing the urgency of directly realizing them. For details about the actual content of the truths, we have to look elsewhere, and other chapters of the Saṃyutta Nikāya provide us with the material we require.

It is noteworthy in this respect that the Buddha's discourses, as found in the Pāli Canon, are linked through a complex network of allusions and cross-references. A theme or topic treated briefly in one place may be elaborated elsewhere; a term used in one sutta may be analyzed and unpacked in another. For example, a sutta on the noble eightfold path (such as SN 45:8) identifies "right mindfulness" with the four establishments of mindfulness and offers a stock formula defining it, but it does not explain what these four modes of developing mindfulness actually involve in practice. For a fuller explanation we have to consult another sutta (DN 22 or MN 10), which describes the practice in detail.

Accordingly, we can see the four noble truths enunciated as a set in the Saccasaṃyutta to be pointing toward other chapters in the Saṃyutta Nikāya for fuller treatment. The formula for the first noble truth states that the noble truth of suffering consists in the five clinging-aggregates (see **1.4**). For a fuller account of the five aggregates, and thus of the first noble truth, we would turn to the Khandhasaṃyutta (SN 22). I have taken a selection of suttas from the Khandhasaṃyutta to make up chapter 2, which I subtitle "the meaning of suffering in brief," echoing the words of the first discourse: *saṃkhittena pañcupādānakkhandhā dukkhā*.

Another sutta on the four noble truths (SN 56:14) defines the first noble truth as the six internal sense bases. Since it is through the six sense bases that all the other phenomena included in the five aggregates arise—feeling, perception, volition, and consciousness—I have designated the sense bases "the channels through which suffering originates." Selected suttas from the Saḷāyatanasaṃyutta (SN 35) therefore make up chapter 3 of this book.

Many discourses state that craving is the origin of suffering, yet this declaration is not explicated in the suttas on the four noble truths. The statement seems to be an oblique way of pointing to an intricate process involving the interplay of a multiplicity of factors. In the Nikāyas we find these factors fused into a lengthy chain that lays bare the causal dynamics that underlie the round of repeated birth and death and thus the genesis of dukkha. This chain is expressed by the formula of dependent origination (*paṭiccasamuppāda*), which usually consists of twelve terms joined by relations of conditionality. The chain situates craving in the middle. At the head of the chain we find ignorance, the most fundamental root, from which emerges a string of factors leading up to craving; and from craving the chain continues further until it culminates in old age and death and all the expressions of existential distress encountered in the course of life, summed up as "sorrow, lamentation, pain, dejection, and misery."

Suttas on dependent origination are collected in the Nidānasaṃyutta (SN 12), a selection from which makes up chapter 4 of the present work. Here it will be seen that the chain of conditions occurs in two modes. One is the mode of origination, which corresponds to the truth of the origin of suffering and shows how each factor gives rise to its successor. The other is the mode of cessation, which corresponds to the truth of the cessation of suffering and shows how removing the condition eliminates its effect.

The fourth noble truth, according to the Buddha's first discourse, is the noble eightfold path, described as "the way to the cessation of suffering." But while the eightfold path may be the most comprehensive and best-known formulation of the path—including as it does cognitive, ethical, and meditative factors—it is not the only set of practices that the Buddha taught as the way to the final goal of his teaching. Rather, he presented the path from different perspectives, governed by the needs and aptitudes of the people being taught. The broadest scheme lays out a group of seven sets of factors containing altogether thirty-seven principles called in Pāli the *bodhipakkhiyā dhammā*, "the aids to enlightenment" or, more poetically, "the wings to awakening." These seven sets, partly overlapping, are: the four establishments of mindfulness, the four right kinds of striving, the four bases for spiritual power, the five faculties, the five powers, the seven factors of enlightenment, and the noble eightfold path. Chapters on each of these have been collected in the last volume of the Saṃyutta Nikāya, the Mahāvagga, the Great Division, which might have also been called the Maggavagga, the Division on the Path.

Chapter 5 of the present work is devoted to texts on the path of practice. If, however, I had attempted to include here suttas representing all seven groups, this would have strained the limits imposed on this volume. I have therefore restricted my choice to suttas drawn from three groups: the four establishments of mindfulness, the seven factors of enlightenment, and the noble eightfold path.

Since the systematic cultivation of mindfulness might be called the essential practice of the way to liberation, I begin with suttas from the Satipaṭṭhānasaṃyutta (SN 47). When mindfulness reaches a certain degree of maturity, it becomes the first of the seven factors of enlightenment, the starting point from which the other six factors emerge; thus suttas from the Bojjhaṅgasaṃyutta (SN 46) constitute the second section of this chapter. And when the seven factors of enlightenment reach their pinnacle, they bring into being the liberating eightfold path, the truly noble path, and thus suttas from the Maggasaṃyutta (SN 45) constitute the third section of this chapter.

The goal of the path is nibbāna. Nibbāna has already been indicated obliquely in the chapter on the four noble truths as the cessation of suffering. Again, it is implied in the chapter on dependent origination as the cessation of each of the links in the formula of dependent origination. Nevertheless, in those chapters it has not been shown explicitly in its own nature. To provide a fuller picture of the goal of the teaching, I have included, as chapter 6, a selection from the Asaṅkhatasaṃyutta (SN 43), the Connected Discourses on the Unconditioned, which offers thirty-two epithets for the goal, with nibbāna being only one of them. Each of these is equated with the destruction of lust, the destruction of hatred, and the destruction of delusion, to be reached by various avenues of practice, elaborately laid down in this chapter.

At the conclusion of many suttas in the Nikāyas, when the Buddha has finished his discourse to an inquirer, the inquirer responds with a stock statement of appreciation: "Excellent, Master Gotama, excellent, Master Gotama! Just as one would turn upright what had been overturned, or would reveal what was concealed, or would point out the path to one who is lost, or would hold up an oil lamp in the darkness, thinking, 'Those with eyes will see forms,' just so the Dhamma has been revealed in many ways by Master Gotama."

My hope is that readers of the present volume will echo this exclamation of delight and then dive more deeply into the Dhamma, both as a fascinating field of study and as a path to a meaningful and fulfilling life.

Sources and Citations

I have used as my basic source for the Pāli texts the electronic version of the Chaṭṭha Saṅgāyana Tipiṭaka (version 4.0), which is based on the printed edition resulting from the Sixth Buddhist Council held in Myanmar in 1956. Occasionally, however, I have adopted an alternative reading found either in the Pali Text Society's Roman-script edition or in the Sri Lankan Buddha Jayanti Sinhala-script edition. Since my purpose here is simply to present a translation of an acceptable version of the texts, I have not attempted to construct a critical edition and thus I have not commented on the variant readings in my notes.

Source references following the title of each selection cite the chapter number of the Saṃyutta followed by the number of the sutta within that chapter. I follow the numbering scheme used in my published translation of the Saṃyutta Nikāya, *The Connected Discourses of the Buddha.* This is followed by the volume and page number of the PTS edition of the Pāli text. Thus "SN 56:1; V 414" is Saṃyutta Nikāya, chapter 56, sutta 1, found in volume V, page 414 of the PTS edition. The numbering of suttas in the Saḷāyatanasaṃyutta (chapter 35) occasionally differs across the different editions of this volume, depending on whether the discourses in a group are considered a single sutta or separate suttas. In chapter 3 of this book I have used the numbering scheme of the *Connected Discourses,* which differs from that of the PTS edition of the Pāli text. Hence in the detailed list of contents and again in chapter 3, I give the sutta number of the PTS edition in brackets following my own number.

The same principle of numbering applies to references to other Nikāyas in the notes. While in my translations of full Nikāyas I have provided many long and detailed explanatory notes, in this book, in order to let the suttas speak for themselves, I have tried to keep the notes to a minimum. Many of my notes refer to the commentary to the Saṃyutta Nikāya, titled the *Sāratthappakāsinī* (Spk). This was written by the Indian monk Buddhaghosa, who came to Sri Lanka in the fifth century to compose commentaries to the four Nikāyas and perhaps other canonical texts. His commentaries were not original works expressing his personal interpretations but were based on older commentaries, no longer extant, that had been preserved in Sri Lanka in the ancient Sinhala language. His main task, as he saw it, was to draw out the explanations found in the ancient commentaries, remove redundancies, and translate the explanations into the language of the canonical texts. His purpose, presumably, was to make the commentaries intelligible to monastics living beyond Sri Lanka.

The book also contains a Pāli-English glossary. This has not been arranged in alphabetical order—whether according to the Pāli alphabet or the English alphabet—but according to the order of the chapters in this book. It provides only the Pāli terms for the key components in each chapter.

I would like to thank John Kelly for help with the proofreading and the staff at Wisdom Publications for another fine job of production.

1. The Four Noble Truths: The Matrix of the Teaching

Introduction

In his first discourse, known as the *Dhammacakkappavattana Sutta*, "The Discourse Setting in Motion the Wheel of the Dhamma," the Buddha spoke of the four noble truths and the noble eightfold path, the unique "middle way" that avoids the dismal ends of sensual indulgence and painful ascetic practices and leads to the peace and freedom of nibbāna. The transmission of the Dhamma hinged upon insight into this interlocking set of principles. It was by comprehending these truths that his first disciples, the five monks, gained the "dust-free, stainless eye of the Dhamma," the decisive breakthrough that opens the liberating path. Repeatedly, during his teaching career, he brought his discourse to a climax with an exposition of the truths.

The four noble truths were so central to the Buddha's exposition of the Dhamma that the compilers of the Saṃyutta Nikāya devoted an entire chapter to this topic, the last in the whole collection. However, the four truths might be seen not merely as one Buddhist doctrine among others, but more broadly as the implicit framework of the whole teaching. The Buddha's chief disciple, Sāriputta, underscored the importance of this formula when he said: "Just as the footprints of all other animals of the jungle can fit into the footprint of an elephant, which is declared chief with respect to size, so whatever wholesome teachings there are can all fit into the four noble truths" (MN 28, I 184). The classical Buddhist commentaries follow up on this suggestion by showing that the four noble truths can be extracted from other teachings even when they are not explicitly mentioned as such.

Modern exponents of Buddhism often assume that the four noble truths are an elementary teaching intended for newcomers to the Dhamma, but the Buddha himself did not treat them in such a way. Rather, he saw them as suitable only for those whose minds were ripe enough to understand them clearly and directly. He would usually begin a discourse to inquirers with a talk on generosity and morality, virtues that any person of moral convictions could appreciate. From there he would proceed to explain the workings of kamma and the realms of rebirth to which different courses of action lead. Then, having described the joys of the heavens, he would speak about the faults in the pursuit of sensual pleasures and the benefits of renunciation, thereby instilling in his audience respect for the kind of contemplative life that he himself had adopted. It was only at this point, when he knew that the minds of his listeners were sufficiently open, trusting, and free from obstructions, that he would reveal the four noble truths, which the texts describe as "the special Dhamma teaching of the buddhas" (*buddhānaṃ sāmukkaṃsikā dhammadesanā*).[2]

The four noble truths might also be seen as the underlying blueprint of the Saṃyutta Nikāya, as explained in the general introduction. The other major chapters of this collection can then be seen as elaborations of the individual truths. It might then be significant that the entire Saṃyutta ends with the chapter on the four noble truths, highlighting this teaching as the crown jewel of this major compilation.

According to **1.10**, the things that the Buddha directly knew were many, like the leaves in a forest grove, but the things he expounded were few, like the leaves he took up in his hand. These few things were suffering, its origin, its cessation, and the path. The reason he did not disclose all the things he had seen was because those things do not bring true benefits. The reason he repeatedly expounded the four noble truths was because these principles are beneficial and lead "to disenchantment, to dispassion, to cessation, to peace, to direct knowledge, to enlightenment, to nibbāna."

The first discourse, the *Dhammacakkappavattana Sutta*, provides formal explanations of the four noble truths.[3] Most of these explanations are also included in **1.4**, which differs from the first discourse only by offering a crisper definition of the first noble truth. In the first discourse, the Buddha enumerates eight kinds of dukkha. The first four—birth, old age, sickness, and death—can be grouped under the heading of physiological suffering. The next three are union with the unpleasant, separation from the pleasant, and not getting what one wants, which can be comprised under the heading of psychological suffering. And the last is the five clinging-aggregates, which might be described as ontological or existential suffering. Omitting the detailed manifestations of dukkha mentioned in the first discourse, text **1.4** defines the first truth simply as the five clinging-aggregates, which in the first discourse are said to encapsulate the truth of suffering "in brief" (*saṃkhittena*).[4]

The Pāli word *dukkha*, common to all four truths, calls for some explanation, necessary to avoid misunderstanding. As a matter of convenience, most translators render this word as "suffering," and I follow their precedent. This rendering, however, can lead to the misunderstanding that the Buddha holds that all existence is perpetually rife with pain and misery. That is not the case at all, for which reason some translators prefer to leave *dukkha* untranslated. In certain contexts, especially in relation to feeling, *dukkha* does mean pain and suffering, and this seems to have been the original usage of the word. However, the Buddha drew this word out from its original context and gave it a deeper significance, using it to highlight the inescapably flawed, deficient, and unsatisfactory nature of sentient existence.

From this perspective, not only painful experience, but *all experience* within the conditioned world is inherently defective. Life, according to the Nikāyas, certainly contains abundant opportunities for joy and happiness, even occasions of rapture and bliss. The popular *Maṅgala Sutta* enumerates thirty-eight blessings, among them such mundane sources of happiness as supporting one's parents, maintaining a family, helping friends and relatives, working at an honest occupation, and engaging in righteous deeds. All these blessings, however, are unstable and subject to change. Every factor of being—every facet of experience—when looked at closely, turns out to be impermanent and therefore unreliable, unable to provide complete satisfaction. It is this sense of deficiency or "lack" that the word *dukkha* is intended to suggest. Ultimate release from dukkha can only be found in that which lies beyond the sphere of transience and mortality—that is, in nibbāna, the unconditioned state free from birth, decay, and death.

The German monk Nyanatiloka, in his classic *The Word of the Buddha*, eloquently captures this meaning of *dukkha* when he writes:

> The term "suffering" (*dukkha*), in the first noble truth, refers therefore not merely to painful bodily and mental sensations due to unpleasant impressions, but it comprises in addition everything productive of suffering or liable to it. The truth of suffering teaches that, owing to the universal law of impermanence, even high and sublime states of happiness are subject to change and destruction, and that all states of existence are therefore unsatisfactory, without exception carrying in themselves the seeds of suffering.[5]

The first noble truth gains further traction from the connection between dukkha and saṃsāra, the round of repeated birth and death. Again, Nyanatiloka astutely points to this connection:

> Saṃsāra is the unbroken sequence of the fivefold *khandha*-combinations [the five aggregates], which, constantly changing from moment to moment, follow continually one upon the other through inconceivable periods of time. Of this saṃsāra a single lifetime constitutes only a tiny fraction. Hence, to be able to comprehend the first noble truth, one must let one's gaze rest upon the saṃsāra, upon this frightful sequence of rebirths, and not merely upon one single lifetime, which of course may sometimes be not very painful.[6]

The origin of dukkha, in the analysis of the four truths, is said to be *taṇhā*, a word translated as "craving" but which literally means "thirst," a blind thirst for pleasure, existence, and even annihilation that operates in the minds of all unenlightened beings. The formula for the second noble truth describes craving as *ponobhavikā*, "causing renewed existence." This underscores the point that craving is the origin of dukkha not only in the immediate psychological sense that insatiable desire breeds frustration, disappointment, and discontent, but in the subtler, deeper sense that craving sustains the cycle of repeated birth and death and thereby underlies all the suffering that arises consequent upon birth. Supported and nurtured by fundamental ignorance, craving propels us through saṃsāra in a blind quest for final satisfaction through the indulgence of self-centered desire. At death, so long as craving has not been expelled, it will drive the stream of consciousness forward into a new birth, and onward from one life to the next. This is the "long journey" on which we have embarked and which, according to the texts, has been proceeding without a discoverable temporal beginning.

The overcoming of dukkha requires that craving be uprooted in its entirety, an attainment that the third noble truth declares a real possibility. Dukkha comes to an end with "the remainderless fading away and cessation of that same craving," the craving that maintains the round of rebirths. And the fourth noble truth reveals the means for reaching this attainment, the noble eightfold path, which will be explored more fully in chapter 5.

Text **1.9** assigns specific tasks to each of the four noble truths, in this respect echoing the middle portion of the first discourse. The truth of suffering is *to be fully understood*; the truth of its origin, craving, is *to be abandoned*; the truth of its cessation is *to be realized* through the eradication of craving; and the truth of the way, the noble eightfold path, is *to be developed* by practice. The four tasks define the work to be undertaken by a disciple on the path. The development of the noble eightfold path brings all four tasks to completion. Such development culminates in the full understanding of dukkha, the abandonment of craving, and the realization of the cessation of dukkha. One who has completed these four tasks can boldly proclaim: "What had to be done has been done" (*kataṃ karaṇīyaṃ*).

The four noble truths served the Buddha not only as a teaching device but as the objects of cultivation and realization. When describing his own attainment of enlightenment, he brings the exposition to its high point by declaring that in the last watch of the night: "When my concentrated mind was purified, bright, unblemished, rid of imperfection, malleable, wieldy, steady, and attained to imperturbability, I directed it to knowledge of the destruction of the influxes. I directly knew as it actually is: 'This is suffering, this its origin, this its cessation, and this the way leading to its cessation.'" With the arising of this insight, "Ignorance was banished and clear knowledge arose, darkness was banished and light arose," and his mind was liberated from the *āsavas*, the primordial "influxes" that sustain the round of rebirths.[7]

In several suttas the Buddha generalizes from his own experience to highlight the centrality of the four noble truths to the attainment of enlightenment and liberation throughout all periods of time, thus universalizing their significance. Text **1.2** states that all those who attain full enlightenment do so by becoming fully enlightened to the four noble truths. The verb used in this passage, *abhisambujjhati*, seems to occur solely in descriptions of a buddha's enlightenment, in contrast to that of his disciples; thus the text is implicitly saying that all buddhas—past, present, and future—become enlightened to these same four truths. Other suttas not included here reinforce this point in relation to the enlightenment of the disciples. SN 56:3 says that all those who rightly go forth into the homeless life do so for the purpose of realizing the four noble truths as they really are, and SN 56:4 says that all those who have rightly gone forth and realized things as they really are, realize the four noble truths as they really are.

Lack of knowledge of the four noble truths is the blind spot—the fundamental ignorance—that underlies craving and thereby keeps beings bound to the round of birth and death. Because they have not seen these truths, beings run pointlessly from one existence to the next, passing through the repetitive cycle of birth, aging, and death, and then on to still another birth. Just as a stick thrown into the air falls sometimes on its bottom, sometimes on its top, so sentient beings who have not seen the four truths, being "hindered by ignorance and fettered by craving," migrate up and down among the multiple realms of existence (**1.11**). Prospects for rebirth are not always bright, but often lead downward to the lower world, where "mutual devouring occurs, the devouring of the weak." Once one is reborn there, we learn from **1.17**, it is hard to regain the human state—as hard as it is for a blind turtle to come across and stick its head through a yoke with a hole floating on the ocean. It is because we have not penetrated the four noble truths, **1.5** tells us, that we have roamed through this "long journey" of saṃsāra, and it is with the penetration of these truths that the wearisome journey comes to an end.

Even seekers dedicated to the pursuit of liberation fail to achieve their aim if they do not understand the four truths. According to **1.15**, those ascetics and brahmins who do not understand these truths "generate volitional activities" that lead to birth, old age, and death, and because they generate these volitional activities, they fall down "the deep precipice" of birth, old age, and death, meeting anguish and misery. It is only when the four truths are directly seen that one stops engaging in these volitional activities, and it is only then that one avoids the fall down the steep precipice.

The purpose of the Buddha's appearance in the world—indeed, the reason for the appearance of any buddha—is to proclaim the four noble truths. So long as a buddha has not appeared, says **1.14**, the world is enveloped in spiritual darkness, the darkness of ignorance. The world is then like the earth before the sun and moon have appeared, when even day and night cannot be distinguished. But when a buddha arises, he is like the sun rising in the sky, shedding its light over the world. With his arising, the darkness of ignorance is dispelled and there is "the explaining, teaching, proclaiming, establishing, disclosing, analyzing, and elucidation of the four noble truths."

Realization of the four noble truths usually comes as the culmination of a rigorous course of training involving ethical conduct, right thinking, meditative concentration, and direct insight. Therefore the Buddha instructs the monks not to indulge in wrong thinking—in thoughts connected with sensuality, ill will, and harmfulness—but to think instead about the four noble truths (**1.2**). They are not only to reflect on the truths but to develop concentration (*samādhi*) as a basis for seeing them with direct vision (**1.1**). He insists they undertake this task with a compelling sense of urgency, just as a person whose turban were on fire would make an urgent effort to extinguish the flames (see **1.12**). Just as it is impossible to construct the upper story of a house without having first constructed the lower story, so **1.16** says, without penetrating these truths it is impossible to make an end of suffering. For this reason, the Buddha constantly presses his disciples to make the effort to realize the four noble truths. Each of the discourses in the Saccasaṃyutta ends with the injunction: "Therefore an exertion should be made [to understand]: 'This is suffering' . . . 'This is the way leading to the cessation of suffering.'"

The initial vision of the four noble truths brings the attainment of stream-entry, the first of the four stages of noble attainment culminating in final liberation.[8] Those who see the four noble truths through this initial breakthrough become "accomplished in view" (*diṭṭhisampanna*) and, as stated in **1.18**, will migrate in the round of rebirths through seven more lives at most. They will not take an eighth existence. But for the Buddha even the attainment of stream-entry is insufficient. The final goal of the path is arahantship, liberation in this very life, which comes about through the destruction of the influxes, the defilements of sensual craving, craving for existence, and ignorance. This, too, according to **1.6**, is attained only by those who directly know the four noble truths. Having made the initial breakthrough, the texts say, one should not pause until one can declare, like the Buddha: "Craving for existence has been cut off; the conduit to existence has been destroyed; now there is no more renewed existence" (**1.5**).

1. *Samādhisutta*
Concentration (SN 56:1; V 414)

"Monks, develop concentration. A concentrated monk understands things as they really are.

"And what does he understand as it really is? He understands as it really is: 'This is suffering.' He understands as it really is: 'This is the origin of suffering.' He understands as it really is: 'This is the cessation of suffering.' He understands as it really is: 'This is the way leading to the cessation of suffering.'

"Monks, develop concentration. A concentrated monk understands things as they really are.

"Therefore, monks, an exertion should be made [to understand]: 'This is suffering.' An exertion should be made [to understand]: 'This is the origin of suffering.' An exertion should be made [to understand]: 'This is the cessation of suffering.' An exertion should be made [to understand]: 'This is the way leading to the cessation of suffering.'"[9]

2. *Samaṇabrāhmaṇasutta*
Ascetics and Brahmins (SN 56:5; V 416–17)

"Whatever ascetics or brahmins in the past, monks, were fully enlightened to things as they really are, they were all fully enlightened to the four noble truths as they really are. Whatever ascetics or brahmins in the future will be fully enlightened to things as they really are, they will all be fully enlightened to the four noble truths as they really are. Whatever ascetics or brahmins now are fully enlightened to things as they really are, they are all fully enlightened to the four noble truths as they really are.

"What four? The noble truth of suffering, the noble truth of the origin of suffering, the noble truth of the cessation of suffering, the noble truth of the way leading to the cessation of suffering. Whatever ascetics or brahmins in the past . . . Whatever ascetics or brahmins in the future . . . Whatever ascetics or brahmins now are fully enlightened to things as they really are, they are all fully enlightened to these four noble truths as they really are.

"Therefore, monks, an exertion should be made [to understand]: 'This is suffering.' An exertion should be made [to understand]: 'This is the origin of suffering.' An exertion should be made [to understand]: 'This is the cessation of suffering.' An exertion should be made [to understand]: This is the way leading to the cessation of suffering.'"

3. *Vitakkasutta*
Thought (SN 56:7; V 417–18)

"Monks, do not think bad, unwholesome thoughts—that is, sensual thought, thought of ill will, thought of harming. For what reason? These thoughts are unbeneficial; they do not pertain to the basis for the spiritual life; they do not lead to disenchantment, to dispassion, to cessation, to peace, to direct knowledge, to enlightenment, to nibbāna.

"When you think, monks, you should think: 'This is suffering'; you should think: 'This is the origin of suffering'; you should think: 'This is the cessation of suffering'; you should think: 'This is the way leading to the cessation of suffering.' For what reason? These thoughts are beneficial; they pertain to the basis for the spiritual life; they lead to disenchantment, to dispassion, to cessation, to peace, to direct knowledge, to enlightenment, to nibbāna.

"Therefore, monks, an exertion should be made [to understand]: 'This is suffering.' . . . 'This is the way leading to the cessation of suffering.'"

4. *Khandhasutta*
Aggregates (SN 56:13; V 425–26)

"There are, monks, these four noble truths. What four? The noble truth of suffering, the noble truth of the origin of suffering, the noble truth of the cessation of suffering, the noble truth of the way leading to the cessation of suffering.

"And what, monks, is the noble truth of suffering? 'The five clinging-aggregates,' it should be said—that is, the form clinging-aggregate, the feeling clinging-aggregate, the perception clinging-aggregate, the volitional-activities clinging-aggregate, the consciousness clinging-aggregate. This is called the 'noble truth of suffering.'

"And what, monks, is the noble truth of the origin of suffering? It is this craving causing renewed existence, accompanied by delight and lust, delighting here and there—that is, craving for sensual pleasures, craving for existence, craving for non-existence.[10] This is called the 'noble truth of the origin of suffering.'

"And what, monks, is the noble truth of the cessation of suffering? It is the remainderless fading away and cessation of that same craving, its giving up, relinquishment, freedom from it, non-attachment. This is called the 'noble truth of the cessation of suffering.'

"And what, monks, is the noble truth of the way leading to the cessation of suffering? It is just this noble eightfold path—

that is, right view, right intention, right speech, right action, right livelihood, right effort, right mindfulness, right concentration. This is called the 'noble truth of the way leading to the cessation of suffering.' These are the four noble truths.

"Therefore, monks, an exertion should be made [to understand]: 'This is suffering.' . . . 'This is the way leading to the cessation of suffering.'"

5. *Koṭigāmasutta*
Koṭigāma (SN 56:21; V 431–32)

On one occasion the Blessed One was dwelling among the Vajjis at Koṭigāma.[11] There the Blessed One addressed the monks thus: "Monks, it is because of not understanding and not penetrating the four noble truths that you and I have run and roamed through this long journey [of saṃsāra].

"What four? It is, monks, because of not understanding and not penetrating the noble truth of suffering that you and I have run and roamed through this long journey [of saṃsāra].[12] It is because of not understanding and not penetrating the noble truth of the origin of suffering . . . the noble truth of the cessation of suffering . . . the noble truth of the way leading to the cessation of suffering that you and I have run and roamed through this long journey [of saṃsāra].

"This noble truth of suffering, monks, has been understood and penetrated. This noble truth of the origin of suffering has been understood and penetrated. This noble truth of the cessation of suffering has been understood and penetrated. This noble truth of the way leading to the cessation of suffering has been understood and penetrated. Craving for existence has been cut off; the conduit to existence has been destroyed; now there is no renewed existence."[13]

"Therefore, monks, an exertion should be made [to understand]: 'This is suffering.' . . . 'This is the way leading to the cessation of suffering.'"

This is what the Blessed One said. Having said this, the Fortunate One, the Teacher, further said this:

"Because of not seeing as they are
the four noble truths,

we have wandered through the long course
in the various kinds of births.

"Now these truths have been seen;
the conduit to existence is severed;
cut off is the root of suffering:
now there is no renewed existence."

6. *Āsavakkhayasutta*
Destruction of the Influxes (SN 56:25; V 434)

"Monks, I say that the destruction of the influxes occurs for one knowing, for one seeing, not for one not knowing, not seeing. For one knowing what, for one seeing what, does the destruction of the influxes occur?[14]

"It is, monks, for one knowing and seeing, 'This is suffering,' that the destruction of the influxes occurs. It is for one knowing and seeing, 'This is the origin of suffering' . . . for one knowing and seeing, 'This is the cessation of suffering' . . . for one knowing and seeing, 'This is the way leading to the cessation of suffering,' that the destruction of the influxes occurs. It is for one knowing thus, for one seeing thus, that the destruction of the influxes occurs.

"Therefore, monks, an exertion should be made [to understand]: 'This is suffering.' . . . 'This is the way leading to the cessation of suffering.'"

7. *Tathasutta*
Real (SN 56:27; V 435)

"There are, monks, these four noble truths. What four? The noble truth of suffering, the noble truth of the origin of suffering, the noble truth of the cessation of suffering, the noble truth of the way leading to the cessation of suffering. These four noble truths are real, not unreal, not otherwise;[15] therefore they are called 'noble truths.'

"Therefore, monks, an exertion should be made [to understand]: 'This is suffering.' . . . 'This is the way leading to the cessation of suffering.'"

8. *Lokasutta*
The World (SN 56:28; V 435)

"There are, monks, these four noble truths. . . . In the world with its devas, with Māra, with Brahmā, in this population with its ascetics and brahmins, with its devas and humans, the Tathāgata is the noble one; therefore they are called 'noble truths.'

"Therefore, monks, an exertion should be made [to understand]: 'This is suffering.' . . . 'This is the way leading to the cessation of suffering.'"

9. *Pariññeyyasutta*
To Be Fully Understood (SN 56:29; V 436)

"Monks, there are these four noble truths. . . . Of these four noble truths, there is a noble truth to be fully understood, a noble truth to be abandoned, a noble truth to be realized, and a noble truth to be developed.

"And what, monks, is the noble truth that is to be fully understood? The noble truth of suffering is to be fully understood; the noble truth of the origin of suffering is to be abandoned; the noble truth of the cessation of suffering is to be realized; the noble truth of the way leading to the cessation of suffering is to be developed.

"Therefore, monks, an exertion should be made [to understand]: 'This is suffering.' . . . 'This is the way leading to the cessation of suffering.'"

10. *Siṃsapāvanasutta*
The Siṃsapā Grove (SN 56:31; V 437–38)

On one occasion the Blessed One was dwelling at Kosambī in a siṃsapā grove. Then the Blessed One took a few siṃsapā leaves with his hand and addressed the monks: "What do you think about this, monks, which is more numerous: these few siṃsapā leaves that I have taken with my hand or those above in the siṃsapā grove?"

"Bhante, the siṃsapā leaves that the Blessed One has taken in his hand are few, but those above in the siṃsapā grove are indeed more numerous."

"So too, monks, that which I have directly known but have not expounded to you is more numerous. And why, monks, have I not expounded this? Because this is unbeneficial; this does not pertain to the basis for the spiritual life; this does not lead to disenchantment, to dispassion, to cessation, to peace, to direct knowledge, to enlightenment, to nibbāna. Therefore I have not expounded it.

"And what, monks, have I expounded? I have expounded: 'This is suffering.' I have expounded: 'This is the origin of suffering.' I have expounded: 'This is the cessation of suffering.' I have expounded: 'This is the way leading to the cessation of suffering.' And why, monks, have I expounded this? Because this is beneficial; this pertains to the basis for the spiritual life; this leads to disenchantment, to dispassion, to cessation, to peace, to direct knowledge, to enlightenment, to nibbāna. Therefore I have expounded this.

"Therefore, monks, an exertion should be made [to understand]: 'This is suffering.' . . . 'This is the way leading to the cessation of suffering.'"

11. *Daṇḍasutta*
The Stick (SN 56:33; V 439–40)

"Just as, monks, a stick, thrown up into the air, sometimes falls on its bottom and sometimes falls on its top, just so, monks, beings hindered by ignorance and fettered by craving, running and roaming, sometimes go from this world to the other world, and sometimes come from the other world to this world. For what reason? Because, monks, they have not seen the four noble truths. What four? The noble truth of suffering . . . the noble truth of the way leading to the cessation of suffering.

"Therefore, monks, an exertion should be made [to understand]: 'This is suffering.' . . . 'This is the way leading to the cessation of suffering.'"

12. *Celasutta*
The Turban (SN 56:34; V 440)

"If, monks, one's turban or head were ablaze, what should be done?"

"If, Bhante, one's turban or head were ablaze, one should practice extraordinary desire, effort, zeal, enthusiasm, persistence, mindfulness, and clear comprehension for extinguishing that [fire on one's] turban or head."

"If, monks, one's turban or head were ablaze one might observe this with equanimity and give it no attention, but so long as the four noble truths have not been realized, one should practice extraordinary desire, effort, zeal, enthusiasm, courage, mindfulness, and clear comprehension for realizing them as they really are.

"Therefore, monks, an exertion should be made [to understand]: 'This is suffering.' . . . 'This is the way leading to the cessation of suffering.'"

13. *Suriyasutta*—1
The Sun—1 (SN 56:37; V 442)

"This, monks, is the forerunner, this is the sign of the rising of the sun—that is, the break of dawn. Just so, for a monk, this is the forerunner, this is the sign for the breakthrough to the four noble truths as they really are—that is, right view.

"Therefore, monks, an exertion should be made [to understand]: 'This is suffering.' . . . 'This is the way leading to the cessation of suffering.'"

14. *Suriyasutta*—2
The Sun—2 (SN 56:38; V 442–43)

"So long, monks, as the sun and moon do not arise in the world, for just so long there is no manifestation of great light and great radiance, but then there is blind darkness, darkness and gloom. For just so long nights and days are not discerned, months and fortnights are not discerned, seasons and years are not discerned.

"But, monks, when the sun and moon arise in the world, then there is the manifestation of great light and great radiance. Then there is no blinding darkness, no darkness and gloom. Then nights and days are discerned, months and fortnights are discerned, seasons and years are discerned.

"So too, monks, so long as the Tathāgata does not arise in

the world, the arahant, the perfectly enlightened one, for just so long there is no manifestation of great light and great radiance, but then there is blinding darkness, darkness and gloom. For just so long there is no explaining, teaching, conveying, establishing, disclosing, analyzing, and elucidation of the four noble truths.

"But, monks, when the Tathāgata arises in the world, the arahant, the perfectly enlightened one, then there is the manifestation of great light and great radiance. Then there is no blinding darkness, no darkness and gloom. Then there is the explaining, teaching, conveying, establishing, disclosing, analyzing, and elucidation of the four noble truths.

"Therefore, monks, an exertion should be made [to understand]: 'This is suffering.' . . . 'This is the way leading to the cessation of suffering.'"

15. *Papātasutta*
The Precipice (SN 56:42; V 448–50)

On one occasion the Blessed One was dwelling at Rājagaha on Mount Vulture Peak. Then the Blessed One addressed the monks thus: "Come, monks, let us go to Paṭibhāna Peak to pass the day."

"Yes, Bhante," those monks replied. Then the Blessed One, together with a number of monks, went to Paṭibhāna Peak. One monk saw the steep precipice off Paṭibhāna Peak and said to the Blessed One: "That precipice is indeed steep, Bhante; that precipice is extremely frightful. But is there, Bhante, any other precipice steeper and more frightful than that one?"

"There is, monk."

"But what, Bhante, is the precipice steeper and more frightful than that one?"

[1. Those who fall down the precipice]
"Those ascetics and brahmins, monks, who do not understand as it really is: 'This is suffering'; who do not understand as it really is: 'This is the origin of suffering'; who do not understand as it really is: 'This is the cessation of suffering'; who do not understand as it really is: 'This is the way leading to the cessation of suffering': they delight in volitional activities that

lead to birth; they delight in volitional activities that lead to old age; they delight in volitional activities that lead to death; they delight in volitional activities that lead to sorrow, lamentation, pain, dejection, and misery.[16]

"Delighted with volitional activities that lead to birth, delighted with volitional activities that lead to old age, delighted with volitional activities that lead to death, delighted with volitional activities that lead to sorrow, lamentation, pain, dejection, and misery, they generate volitional activities that lead to birth; they generate volitional activities that lead to old age; they generate volitional activities that lead to death; they generate volitional activities that lead to sorrow, lamentation, pain, dejection, and misery.

"Having generated volitional activities that lead to birth, having generated volitional activities that lead to old age, having generated volitional activities that lead to death, having generated volitional activities that lead to sorrow, lamentation, pain, dejection, and misery, they fall down the precipice of birth; they fall down the precipice of old age; they fall down the precipice of death; they fall down the precipice of sorrow, lamentation, pain, dejection, and misery.

"They are not freed from birth, from old age, from death, from sorrow, from lamentation, from pain, from dejection, from misery. 'They are not freed from suffering,' I say.

[2. Those who do not fall down the precipice]

"But, monks, those ascetics or brahmins who understand as it really is: 'This is suffering' . . . who understand as it really is: 'This is the way leading to the cessation of suffering': they do not delight in volitional activities that lead to birth. . . . Not delighted with volitional activities that lead to birth, they do not generate volitional activities that lead to birth. . . . Not having generated volitional activities that lead to birth . . . they do not fall down the precipice of birth; they do not fall down the precipice of old age; they do not fall down the precipice of death; they do not fall down the precipice of sorrow, lamentation, pain, dejection, and misery.

"They are freed from birth, from old age, from death, from sorrow, from lamentation, from pain, from dejection, from misery. 'They are freed from suffering,' I say.

"Therefore, monks, an exertion should be made [to understand]: 'This is suffering.' . . . 'This is the way leading to the cessation of suffering.'"

16. *Kūṭāgārasutta*
Peaked House (SN 56:44; V 452–53)

"If, monks, one would say thus, 'Without having realized the noble truth of suffering as it really is . . . without having realized the noble truth of the way leading to the cessation of suffering as it really is, I will completely make an end of suffering,' there is no possibility of this.

"Suppose, monks, someone would say thus: 'Without having built the lower story of a peaked house, I will set up the upper story'; there is no possibility of this. Just so, monks, though someone would say thus: 'Without having realized the noble truth of suffering as it really is . . . without having realized the noble truth of the way leading to the cessation of suffering as it really is, I will completely make an end of suffering,' there is no possibility of this.

"But, monks, if one would say thus, 'Having realized the noble truth of suffering as it really is . . . having realized the noble truth of the way leading to the cessation of suffering as it really is, I will completely make an end of suffering,' there is this possibility.

"Suppose, monks, one would say: 'Having built the lower story of a peaked house, I will set up the upper story'; there is this possibility. Just so, monks, if one would say thus: 'Having realized the noble truth of suffering as it really is . . . having realized the noble truth of the way leading to the cessation of suffering as it really is, I will completely make an end of suffering,' there is this possibility.

"Therefore, monks, an exertion should be made [to understand]: 'This is suffering.' . . . 'This is the way leading to the cessation of suffering.'"

17. *Chiggaḷayugasutta*
Yoke with a Hole (SN 56:47; V 455–56)

"Suppose, monks, a man would throw a yoke with a single

hole into the great ocean, and there was a blind turtle that would come to the surface once every hundred years. What do you think, monks, would that blind turtle, coming to the surface once every hundred years, insert its neck into that yoke with a single hole?"

"If ever, Bhante, surely it would be after the passage of a long period of time."

"I say, monks, that blind turtle, coming to the surface once every hundred years, would more quickly insert its neck into that yoke with a single hole than the fool who has gone once to the lower world would regain the human state.

"For what reason? Because here there is no Dhamma conduct, no righteous conduct, no wholesome activity, no meritorious activity. Here mutual devouring occurs, the devouring of the weak. For what reason? Because of not having seen the four noble truths. What four? The noble truth of suffering . . . the noble truth of the way leading to the cessation of suffering.

"Therefore, monks, an exertion should be made [to understand]: 'This is suffering.' . . . 'This is the way leading to the cessation of suffering.'"

18. *Sinerupabbatarājasutta*
Sineru, King of Mountains (SN 56:49; V 457–58)

"Suppose, monks, a man would place beside Sineru, the king of mountains, seven grains of gravel the size of mung beans. What do you think, monks, which is more: the seven grains of gravel the size of mung beans that have been placed there or Sineru, the king of mountains?"

"This indeed is more, Bhante—that is, Sineru, the king of mountains. The seven grains of gravel the size of mung beans are trifling. Compared to Sineru, the king of mountains, the seven grains of gravel are not even calculable, do not even bear comparison, do not amount even to a fraction."

"Just so, monks, for a noble disciple, a person accomplished in view, one who has made the breakthrough,[17] the suffering that has been destroyed and eliminated is more, while that which remains is trifling. Compared to the former mass of suffering that has been destroyed and eliminated, the latter is not even calculable, does not even bear comparison, does not amount even to a fraction, because there is a maximum of seven more lives for one who understands as it really is: 'This is suffering'; who understands as it really is: 'This is the origin of suffering'; who understands as it really is: 'This is the cessation of suffering'; who understands as it really is: 'This is the way leading to the cessation of suffering.'

"Therefore, monks, an exertion should be made [to understand]: 'This is suffering.' An exertion should be made [to understand]: 'This is the origin of suffering.' An exertion should be made [to understand]: 'This is the cessation of suffering.' An exertion should be made [to understand]: 'This is the way leading to the cessation of suffering.'"

2. The Five Aggregates: The Meaning of Suffering in Brief

Introduction

In his first discourse the Buddha declared, "In brief, the five clinging-aggregates are suffering" (*saṃkhittena pañcupādānakkhandhā dukkhā*). This indicates that the range of dukkha is not confined to experiential pain and distress but extends to all aspects of our being. In this sutta, however, the Buddha did not explain what is meant by the five aggregates, nor did he analyze them at length. For clarification of this matter, we must turn to the Khandhasaṃyutta (SN 22), which serves as an extended commentary on that statement, drawing out the implications concealed within those trenchant words. This *saṃyutta* contains some 150 suttas on the five aggregates, many highly repetitive. Of these, I have selected for this chapter sixteen of the pithiest and most illuminating.

The word *khandha* itself has multiple meanings, among them a mass (of firewood or water), the trunk of a tree, the torso of the body, or the shoulder of an elephant. In the context of the Buddha's teaching, the word refers to five groups into which he classified the constituents of experience: material form, feeling, perception, volitional activities, and consciousness. Each aggregate can be seen as a broad category comprising a multiplicity of factors sharing a particular quality or function. Though experience in its immediacy occurs as a unified whole, in retrospect any experience—any occasion of consciousness—can be reflectively analyzed into these factors.

This use of the term "aggregate" as a category of classification is made explicit in **2.13**. Here, when a monk asks the Buddha how the designation "aggregates" applies to the aggregates, he replies: "Whatever form there is, whether past, future, or present, internal or external, gross or subtle, inferior or superior, far or near: this is called the form aggregate." And so for the other four aggregates. Thus each aggregate includes every instance of the particular factor that gives its name to the category. These instances are distinguished in eleven ways. Three refer to location in time: either past, future, or present. The next dyad refers to position relative to oneself: as pertaining either to oneself or to other beings apart from oneself. Next come two dyads referring to quality—either gross or subtle, and inferior or superior. And finally comes a dyad referring to spatial location, either far or near.

The content of the five aggregates is specified in SN 22:56 (III 59–61), a text not included in the present collection. The Buddha there explains that the aggregate of form (*rūpakkhandha*)—that is, material substance—consists of the four great elements and the form derived from the four great elements. The four great elements are the primary elements of ancient Indian physics—earth, water, fire, and air—which, according to the Pāli commentaries, represent four behavioral properties of matter.[18] The earth element represents solidity or hardness (and its contrary, softness) and has the function of supporting the other elements. The water element represents liquidity and has the function of binding the material particles. The fire element represents heat (and its absence, coolness), with the function of "ripening" matter. And the air element represents distension, occurring in the modes of expansion and contraction. The category of "derived form" includes all kinds of matter derived from the four elements. The most important of these are the space element, the five sense faculties, and the sensory objects—visible form, sound, odor, and taste.[19]

Feeling arises through contact, the encounter of consciousness with an object through a sense base, which can include the purely internal mind base cognizing purely mental objects. The aggregate of feeling (*vedanākkhandha*) includes the six kinds of feeling, each designated after the kind of contact that serves as its condition. Thus there is feeling born of eye-contact, feeling born of ear-contact, feeling born of nose-contact, feeling born of tongue-contact, feeling born of body-contact, and feeling born of mind-contact. In the Buddhist analysis of experience, the term *vedanā* refers strictly to the "affective tone" of an experience, whether pleasant, painful, or neutral. It does not signify emotion, which in terms of the aggregate scheme would likely be considered a complex phenomenon involving the intersection of several aggregates.

The aggregate of perception (*saññākkhandha*), which also arises through contact, consists of the six types of perception. These are designated in relation to their objects rather than their sense faculties: perception of visible forms, perception of sounds, perception of odors, perception of tastes, perception of tactile objects, and perception of mental objects. Perception has the function of singling out and grasping the distinctive qualities of the object, a function that serves as the basis for identification, designation, and subsequent recognition. Some suttas highlight the dangers inherent in raw perception, stemming from its tendency to create and posit inappropriate labels, which result in a distorted, biased, and deceptive picture of the world.

The aggregate of volitional activities (*saṅkhārakkhandha*) comprises the six kinds of volition, also named after their objects: volition regarding visible forms, volition regarding sounds, volition regarding odors, volition regarding tastes, volition regarding tactile objects, and volition regarding mental objects. The function of volition is to instigate action, and thus it is through this aggregate that kamma is created, in accordance with the Buddha's statement: "It is volition, monks, that I call kamma; for having willed, one acts through body, speech, and mind."[20] In Buddhist texts of a slightly later period, the range of this aggregate is expanded so that it serves as a broad category comprising all the varied mental functions mentioned in the suttas that don't fit neatly into the other three mental aggregates. It comes to include, in addition to volition, such factors as thought (*vitakka*) and examination (*vicāra*), such unwholesome states as greed, hatred, and delusion, and such wholesome states as mindfulness, kindness, compassion, and wisdom.

The aggregate of consciousness encompasses the six kinds of consciousness: eye-consciousness, ear-consciousness, nose-consciousness, tongue-consciousness, body-consciousness, and mind-consciousness. The exact distinction between consciousness and perception—between *viññāṇa* and *saññā*—is hard to draw. The two are inextricably linked, and the texts themselves do not clearly differentiate them. However, building upon the fact that perception is distinguished by way of its objects and consciousness by way of its internal sense base,[21] I would stipulate that consciousness is the factor that "illuminates" an entire sensory sphere, making it accessible through a sense faculty, while perception is the factor that homes in on the sense objects illuminated by consciousness, distinguishing and labeling them and ordering them into an intelligible world subsumed under an array of concepts.

The Buddha casts the aggregates in such a major role in his teaching because, in the mental purview of ordinary people, the aggregates serve as the primary basis for clinging. Clinging occurs in a double role, by way of appropriation and identification, the two complementary sides of distorted cognition rooted in fundamental ignorance. In their totality the five aggregates comprise all the things we most intimately take to be "mine"; hence they are the basis for appropriation. At the same time, they constitute the grounds for identification, for the positing of our sense of personal identity. They are the objects on which we impute the innate sense of "I" and reflectively define as our "self."

The five are designated "clinging-aggregates" precisely because they serve as the objects of clinging. While clinging can occur in diverse ways, the most insidious type, according to the Nikāyas, is the attachment to the aggregates as being "mine," "I," and "my self." For the ordinary unenlightened person, these notions seem incontrovertible, even self-evident. We spontaneously take the constituents of body and mind to be "I" and "mine," and then, through reflection on the inherent notion of "I," we posit a "self," a higher-order thesis about our essential identity. We then seek to determine the exact relationship between that apparent self and the material and mental constituents of our being. Since the self is a cipher, an unfindable blank, this leads to an anxious quest to fill in the blank with a concrete content, a project that culminates in a plethora of contesting views about the nature of the self.

Under the sway of distorted cognition, the ordinary person—known as the *puthujjana*, translated here as "worldling"—posits a self existing in some definite relation to the five aggregates. The view of a self is what the suttas call *sakkāyadiṭṭhi*, an expression notoriously hard to translate but which is rendered here with the clunky expression "the view of the personal-assemblage." The "personal-assemblage" (*sakkāya*) is the assemblage of the five aggregates themselves; *sakkāyadiṭṭhi* is the view that arises in relation to this assemblage, asserting the self to be either identical with one or another of the aggregates, or to possess them, or to be contained within them, or to contain them within itself.

Since these four views can be asserted in relation to each of the five aggregates, this entails that there are twenty possible formulations of "the view of the personal-assemblage." These are specified below in **2.13.4**. The worldling might adopt just one of them or try to hold several at the same time, even though they may be incompatible with one another. Just as a dog bound to a post keeps on running around the post, so, according to SN 22:100 (III 150–51), having adopted a view of self, the worldling keeps on revolving around the five aggregates, unable to find release.

The problems inherent in identification with an assumed "self" are compounded by the fact that the five aggregates serve as the basis for pleasure and enjoyment. As **2.5** points out, each of the aggregates can be regarded from three perspectives: by way of the enjoyment it yields, the danger inherent in it, and the way of escape or release from it. The enjoyment consists in the "pleasure and joy" that arise in dependence on the aggregates. We cling to our bodies as the essential instrument for finding happiness and pleasure; we crave pleasant feelings, seek out agreeable objects of perception, launch ambitious projects or engage in enjoyable activities, and hold to consciousness as the precondition for all experience of pleasure. Yet underlying this enjoyment, hidden out of sight, is the danger lurking underfoot: that each of the aggregates is impermanent, unable to give enduring satisfaction, and subject to change.

In recognition of this danger, the Buddha incorporated the five clinging-aggregates into his exposition of the noble truth of suffering. To identify with them as "I" or to appropriate them as "mine" is to expose oneself to suffering when the aggregates change and fail to meet our expectations. To cling to the aggregates is, in effect, to cling to dukkha. Once we recognize the suffering inherent in the five aggregates, we then seek the escape or release from them, which is to be won by "the removal and abandonment of desire-and-lust" in regard to each of the aggregates.

The Buddha's achievement, on the occasion of his enlightenment, was to penetrate the real nature of the five aggregates—which he called "world-phenomena in the world"—and then throughout his teaching career "to point them out, teach them, make them known, establish them, disclose, analyze, and elucidate them" (**2.14**). As the pioneer, the discoverer of the path, he first gains his own release from bondage to the five aggregates; then, on the basis of his own realization, he guides others to liberation. Those who follow his teaching and practice as instructed become "liberated by wisdom," also winning release from the aggregates (**2.8**).

In sounding his message of liberation, the Buddha's proclamation is like a lion's roar. As the lion's roar fills all the other animals with fear and dread, so the Buddha's teaching that the five aggregates undergo origination and dissolution extends throughout the world system. It reaches even to the heavens, filling the powerful deities in the celestial realms with the shocking realization that they too are impermanent (**2.12**).

To break the false identification with the five aggregates, the Buddha proclaims that all these constituents of our being, which we cling to and identify with, are really non-self (*anattā*), not our true identity. Contrary to popular misconception, the Buddha does not explicitly state "there is no self." Rather, he takes a more pragmatic approach, taking up for examination the things assumed to be a self and showing, through reasoned argument, that they fail to measure up to the criteria of true selfhood. Thus *anattā* functions not as a blanket denial of a self but as a negation of the claims made about the things taken to be the self. The entities usually taken up for examination are those contained within the five aggregates. Invariably the conclusion is reached that the five aggregates are not the self they are assumed to be; in other words, they are *anattā*.

The texts offer various approaches to demonstrating the non-self nature of the aggregates. The best-known source for such demonstration is the *Anattalakkhaṇasutta*, "The Discourse on the Non-Self Characteristic" (included here as **2.9**). This is considered the second formal discourse of the Buddha, delivered a week after the first discourse. The sutta proposes two arguments undermining the identification of the aggregates as a self. Both are contingent on certain presuppositions about the nature of selfhood. While these premises concerning the idea of a self may have been shared by various strains of thought in the Indian philosophical culture during the Buddha's time, the sutta's arguments do not require adherence to ancient Indian metaphysics but strike at our innate conviction that there is an autonomous subject of experience residing at the core of our being. Even beneath the threshold of clear awareness, we entertain the intuition that our life revolves around a solid, immutable "I," a center of thought and emotion, the source of volitional activity, giving us the concrete sense of "being somebody." This, in the final analysis, is the target of the Buddha's arguments in advancing his teaching on *anattā*.

The first argument in the "Discourse on Non-Self" is based on the premise that a true self should be invulnerable to pain and suffering. The corollary of this premise holds that the self should be autonomous, able to exert control over itself and over the things that come within its sphere of influence. And a third premise takes the self to be intrinsically permanent. Everything else might change and vanish, but the self persists, ever retaining its intrinsic identity.

The first argument against the notion of a truly existent self takes as its foil the premises of invulnerability and autonomy. It proceeds from the recognition that each aggregate is subject to affliction. The body falls ill and decays, painful feelings harass us throughout the day, disagreeable perceptions assail us, our volitional processes refuse to heed our wishes, and our consciousness flickers and falters, throwing up thoughts, emotions, and impulses that cause us conflict and distress. Being beyond our control—the basis for pain and affliction—the aggregates refuse to conform to our desires, which they would necessarily do if they were truly our self, truly "I" and "mine." Hence it turns out that each of the aggregates is *anattā*, not our self, not "I" or "mine."

The second argument rests on the premise that the self must be permanent and a source of lasting happiness. The argument begins with the empirical observation that the aggregates are all impermanent. Each aggregate, closely examined, is seen to arise and pass away, and, as our powers of observation become ever more acute, the process of arising and passing is seen to be occurring ever more rapidly, at ever subtler levels. Being impermanent, the aggregates cannot be a source of lasting happiness. They are therefore dukkha, defective and unsatisfactory. And since they all turn out to be impermanent, dukkha, and subject to change, they cannot be taken as "mine" or "I" or "my self," for what is truly "my self" must be permanent and blissful.

The three terms of this argument—impermanence, dukkha, and non-self—become the hallmarks of the Buddha's teaching, known as the "three characteristics." They are the marks of things to be penetrated with insight in order to remove the cognitive delusions of permanence, pleasure, and self. In the standard paradigm, insight progresses from impermanence to dukkha, and from impermanence and dukkha together to non-self, the subtlest and deepest of the three. While this three-step progression is the usual procedure the Buddha offers for cutting off identification with the aggregates, other texts offer more direct strategies. Some proceed straight from the impermanence of the aggregates to the destruction of the defilements. Thus **2.1** moves directly from insight into impermanence to detachment and liberation, while **2.2** derives the impermanence of each aggregate from the impermanence of its conditions. Text **2.16** maintains that perception of the aggregates as impermanent "eliminates all sensual lust, eliminates all lust for form, eliminates all lust for existence, eliminates all ignorance, demolishes all conceit 'I am.'"

Other suttas, such as **2.11**, suggest that one can directly contemplate the five aggregates as non-self without proceeding through any of the preliminary steps. Here, a monk named Rādha asks the Buddha how one can eliminate "I-making, mine-making, and tendencies to conceit." The Buddha responds by telling him straightaway to see each of the aggregates in all its manifestations with "correct wisdom" thus: "This is not mine, this I am not, this is not my self."

Text **2.15** exposes the intrinsic emptiness of the five aggregates, comparing them, respectively, to a lump of foam, bubbles on the surface of water, a mirage, a plantain trunk, and a magical illusion. While each of these appear solid to the untrained eye, on inspection they turn out to be void, hollow, and insubstantial. So too, when the aggregates are closely investigated with insight, they turn out to be void, hollow, and insubstantial. While the term "non-self" is not expressly used in this sutta, the implication is clear enough that this is what is intended.

No matter which approach is taken, the culmination is always the same. By seeing into the non-self nature of the aggregates, one becomes disenchanted, losing one's fascination with the aggregates and all the prospects of enjoyment they promise. And then, the texts continue: "Being disenchanted, one becomes dispassionate. Through dispassion one is liberated. In regard to what is liberated, the knowledge occurs thus: 'Liberated.' One understands: 'Finished is birth, the spiritual life has been lived, what had to be done has been done, there is no further for this state of being.'"

Aggregate	*Contents*	*Condition*	*Simile*
form	four great elements and form derived from them	nutriment	a lump of foam
feeling	six classes of feeling: born of contact through eye, ear, nose, tongue, body, and mind	contact	a water bubble
perception	six classes of perception: of forms, sounds, smells, tastes, tactile objects, and mental objects	contact	a mirage
volitional activities	six classes of volition: regarding forms, sounds, smells, tastes, tactile objects, and mental objects	contact	a plantain-tree trunk
consciousness	six classes of consciousness: eye-, ear-, nose-, tongue-, body-, mind-consciousness	name-and-form	a magical illusion

1. *Aniccasutta*
Impermanent (SN 22:12; III 21)

"Form, monks, is impermanent, feeling is impermanent, perception is impermanent, volitional activities are impermanent, consciousness is impermanent.

"Thus seeing, monks, the learned noble disciple becomes disenchanted with form, disenchanted with feeling, disenchanted with perception, disenchanted with volitional activities, disenchanted with consciousness.

"Being disenchanted, he becomes dispassionate. Through dispassion he is liberated. In regard to what is liberated, the knowledge occurs thus: 'Liberated.' He understands: 'Finished is birth, the spiritual life has been lived, what had to be done has been done, there is no further for this state of being.'"

2. *Sahetu-aniccasutta*
Impermanent with Cause (SN 22:18; III 23)

"Form, monks, is impermanent. The cause and condition for the arising of form is also impermanent. How, monks, could form, which has originated from what is impermanent, be permanent?

"Feeling is impermanent. . . . Perception is impermanent. . . . Volitional activities are impermanent. . . . Consciousness is impermanent. The cause and condition for the arising of consciousness is also impermanent. How, monks, could consciousness, which has originated from what is impermanent, be permanent?"

"Thus seeing . . . [he] understands: 'Finished is birth, the spiritual life has been lived, what had to be done has been done, there is no further for this state of being.'"

3. *Pariññasutta*
Full Understanding (SN 22:23; III 26)

"I will teach you, monks, things to be fully understood and full understanding. Listen to that. And what, monks, are things to be fully understood? Form is a thing to be fully understood, feeling is a thing to be fully understood, perception is a thing to be fully understood, volitional activities are things to be fully understood, consciousness is a thing to be fully understood. These are called 'things to be fully understood.'

"And what, monks, is full understanding? The destruction of lust, the destruction of hatred, the destruction of delusion: this is called 'full understanding.'"[22]

4. *Abhijānasutta*
Directly Knowing (SN 22:24; III 26–27)

"One not directly knowing form, monks, not fully understanding it, not removing passion for it, not abandoning it, is incapable of destroying suffering. One not directly knowing feeling . . . not directly knowing perception . . . not directly knowing volitional activities . . . not directly knowing consciousness, not fully understanding it, not removing passion for it, not abandoning it, is incapable of destroying suffering.

"But one directly knowing form, monks, fully understanding it, removing passion for it, abandoning it, is capable of destroying suffering. One directly knowing feeling . . . directly knowing perception . . . directly knowing volitional activities . . . directly knowing consciousness, fully understanding it, removing passion for it, abandoning it, is capable of destroying suffering."

5. *Assādasutta*—1
Enjoyment—1 (SN 22:26; III 27–28)

"Before the enlightenment, monks, while I was just a bodhisatta, not fully enlightened, this occurred to me: 'What is the enjoyment in form, what is the danger, what is the escape? What is the enjoyment in feeling, what is the danger, what is the escape? What is the enjoyment in perception, what is the danger, what is the escape? What is the enjoyment in volitional activities, what is the danger, what is the escape? What is the enjoyment in consciousness, what is the danger, what is the escape?'

"This occurred to me, monks: 'The pleasure and joy that arise in dependence on form: this is the enjoyment in form. That form is impermanent, suffering, and subject to change: this is the danger in form. The removal of desire-and-lust, the abandonment of desire-and-lust, in regard to form: this is the escape from form. The pleasure and joy that arise in dependence on feeling. . . . The pleasure and joy that arise in dependence on perception. . . . The pleasure and joy that arise in dependence on volitional activities. . . . The pleasure and joy that arise in dependence on consciousness: this is the enjoyment in consciousness. That consciousness is impermanent, suffering, and subject to change: this is the danger in consciousness. The removal of desire-and-lust, the abandonment of desire-and-lust, in regard to consciousness: this is the escape from consciousness.'

"So long, monks, as I did not directly know as it really is, in regard to these five clinging-aggregates, the enjoyment as the enjoyment, the danger as the danger, and the escape as the escape, for so long, in the world with its devas, Māra, and Brahmā, in the population with its ascetics and brahmins, its devas and humans, I did not claim: 'I have attained the unsurpassed perfect enlightenment.'

"But when, monks, I directly knew as it really is, in regard to these five clinging-aggregates, the enjoyment as the enjoyment, the danger as the danger, and the escape as the escape, then, in the world with its devas, Māra, and Brahmā, in the population with its ascetics and brahmins, its devas and humans, I claimed: 'I have attained the unsurpassed perfect enlightenment.' And the knowledge and vision arose in me: 'Unshakable is my liberation of mind; this is my final birth; now there is no renewed existence.'"

6. *Assādasutta*—2
Enjoyment—2 (SN 22:28; III 29–31)

"If, monks, there were no enjoyment in form, beings would not become attached to form. But because there is enjoyment in form, beings become attached to form.

"If there were no danger in form, beings would not become disenchanted with form. But because there is danger in form, beings become disenchanted with form.

"If there were no escape from form, beings would not escape from form. But because there is an escape from form, beings escape from form.

"If, monks, there were no enjoyment in feeling . . . no enjoyment in perception . . . no enjoyment in volitional activities . . . no enjoyment in consciousness, beings would not become attached to consciousness. But because there is enjoyment in consciousness, beings become attached to consciousness. If there were no danger in consciousness, beings would not become disenchanted with consciousness. But because there is danger in consciousness, beings become disenchanted with consciousness. If there were no escape from consciousness, beings would not escape from consciousness. But because there is an escape from consciousness, beings escape from consciousness.

"So long, monks, as beings have not directly known as it really is, in regard to these five clinging-aggregates, the enjoyment as enjoyment, the danger as danger, and the escape as escape, for so long, in the world with its devas, Māra, and Brahmā, in the population with its ascetics and brahmins, its devas and humans, beings do not dwell released, detached, freed, with an unbounded mind.

"But when, monks, beings have directly known as it really is, in regard to these five clinging-aggregates, the enjoyment as enjoyment, the danger as danger, and the escape as escape, then, in the world with its devas, Māra, and Brahmā, in the population with its ascetics and brahmins, its devas and humans, beings dwell released, detached, freed, with an unbounded mind."

7. *Natumhākaṃsutta*
Not Yours (SN 22:33; III 33–34)

"Whatever, monks, is not yours, abandon it. When that is abandoned by you, this will be for your welfare and happiness. And what, monks, is not yours? Form is not yours: abandon it. When that is abandoned by you, this will be for your welfare and happiness. Feeling is not yours. . . . Perception is not yours. . . . Volitional activities are not yours. . . . Consciousness is not yours: abandon it. When that is abandoned by you, this will be for your welfare and happiness.

"Suppose, monks, people would remove the grass, logs, branches, and foliage in this Jeta's Grove, or burn them, or do with them as they wish. Would it occur to you thus: 'People are removing us, or burning us, or doing with us as they wish'?"

"Surely not, Bhante. For what reason? Because that is not our self or what belongs to our self."

"Just so, monks, form is not yours: abandon it. When that is abandoned by you, this will be for your welfare and happiness. . . . Consciousness is not yours: abandon it. When that is abandoned by you, this will be for your welfare and happiness."

8. *Sammāsambuddhasutta*
The Perfectly Enlightened One (SN 22:58; III 65–66)

"The Tathāgata, monks, the arahant, the perfectly enlightened one, is liberated by non-clinging through disenchantment with form, through dispassion and cessation, and is called 'a perfectly enlightened one.' A monk liberated by wisdom is also liberated by non-clinging through disenchantment with form, through dispassion and cessation, and is called 'liberated by wisdom.'

"The Tathāgata, the arahant, the perfectly enlightened one, is liberated by non-clinging through disenchantment with feeling . . . through disenchantment with perception . . . through disenchantment with volitional activities . . . through disenchantment with consciousness, through dispassion and cessation, and is called 'a perfectly enlightened one.' A monk liberated by wisdom is also liberated by non-clinging through disenchantment with feeling . . . through disenchantment with perception . . . through disenchantment with volitional activities . . . through disenchantment with consciousness, through dispassion and cessation, and is called 'liberated by wisdom.'

"There, monks, what is the distinction, what is the disparity, what is the difference between the Tathāgata, the arahant, the perfectly enlightened one, and a monk liberated by wisdom?"

"Bhante, for us teachings are rooted in the Blessed One, guided by the Blessed One, take recourse in the Blessed One. Please, Bhante, let the Blessed One clear up the meaning of this statement. Having heard it from him, the monks will retain it in mind."

"In that case, monks, listen and attend well, I will speak."—"Yes, Bhante," the monks replied. The Blessed One said this:

"The Tathāgata, monks, the arahant, the perfectly enlightened one, is the originator of the [previously] unarisen path, the producer of the [previously] unproduced path, the one who declares the [previously] undeclared path; he is the path-knower, the path-finder, the path-expert. And his disciples now dwell as path-followers and become possessed of it later. This, monks, is the distinction, this is the disparity, this is the difference between the Tathāgata, the arahant, the perfectly enlightened one, and a monk liberated by wisdom."

9. *Anattalakkhaṇasutta*
The Non-Self Characteristic (SN 22:59; III 66–68)

[1. The argument from affliction]
On one occasion the Blessed One was dwelling at Bārāṇasī in Isipatana, in the deer park. There the Blessed One addressed the monks of the group of five thus: "Monks!"[23]—"Venerable One!" those monks replied to the Blessed One. The Blessed One said this:

"Form, monks, is non-self. For if, monks, form were self, this form would not lead to affliction, and it would be possible [to exercise control] over form thus:[24] 'Let my form be thus; let my form not be thus.' But because form is non-self, form leads to affliction, and it is not possible [to exercise control] over form thus: 'Let my form be thus; let my form not be thus.'

"Feeling is non-self. . . . Perception is non-self. . . . Volitional activities are non-self. . . . Consciousness is non-self. For if, monks, consciousness were self, this consciousness would not lead to affliction, and it would be possible [to exercise control] over consciousness thus: 'Let my consciousness be thus; let my consciousness not be thus.' But because consciousness is non-self, consciousness leads to affliction, and it is not possible [to exercise control] over consciousness thus: 'Let my consciousness be thus; let my consciousness not be thus.'

[2. The argument from impermanence]
"What do you think, monks, is form permanent or impermanent?"—"Impermanent, Bhante."—"But is that which is impermanent suffering or happiness?"—"Suffering, Bhante."—"But is it fitting to regard that which is impermanent, suffering,

and subject to change thus: 'This is mine, this I am, this is my self'?"—"Surely not, Bhante."

"Is feeling permanent or impermanent?. . . Is perception permanent or impermanent?. . . Are volitional activities permanent or impermanent?. . . Is consciousness permanent or impermanent?"—"Impermanent, Bhante."—"But is that which is impermanent suffering or happiness?"—"Suffering, Bhante."—"But is it fitting to regard that which is impermanent, suffering, and subject to change thus: 'This is mine, this I am, this is my self '?"—"Surely not, Bhante."

"Therefore, monks, whatever form there is, whether past, future, or present, internal or external, gross or subtle, inferior or superior, far or near, all form should be seen as it really is with correct wisdom thus: 'This is not mine, this I am not, this is not my self.'

"Whatever feeling there is. . . . Whatever perception there is. . . . Whatever volitional activities there are. . . . Whatever consciousness there is, whether past, future, or present, internal or external, gross or subtle, inferior or superior, far or near, all consciousness should be seen as it really is with correct wisdom thus: 'This is not mine, this I am not, this is not my self.'

"Seeing thus, monks, the learned noble disciple becomes disenchanted with form, disenchanted with feeling, disenchanted with perception, disenchanted with volitional activities, disenchanted with consciousness. Being disenchanted, he becomes dispassionate. Through dispassion he is liberated. In regard to what is liberated, the knowledge occurs thus: 'Liberated.' He understands: 'Finished is birth, the spiritual life has been lived, what had to be done has been done, there is no further for this state of being.'"

[3. Conclusion]
This is what the Blessed One said. Elated, the monks of the group of five delighted in the Blessed One's statement. And while this discourse was being spoken, through non-clinging the minds of the monks of the group of five were liberated from the influxes.[25]

10. *Upādiyamānasutta*
One Clinging (SN 22:63; III 73–74)

Then a certain monk approached the Blessed One, paid homage to him, and sat down to one side. Seated to one side, that monk said this to the Blessed One: "Please, Bhante, let the Blessed One briefly teach me the Dhamma, so that, having heard the Dhamma from the Blessed One, I might dwell alone, withdrawn, diligent, ardent, and resolute."

"One clinging, monk, is bound to Māra; one not clinging is freed from the Evil One."

"Understood, Blessed One! Understood, Fortunate One!"

"In what way, monk, do you understand in detail the meaning of what was briefly stated by me?"

"One clinging to form, Bhante, is bound by Māra; one not clinging is freed from the Evil One. One clinging to feeling. . . . One clinging to perception. . . . One clinging to volitional activities. . . . One clinging to consciousness is bound by Māra; one not clinging is freed from the Evil One. It is in such a way, Bhante, that I understand in detail the meaning of what was briefly stated by the Blessed One."

"Good, good, monk! It is good that you understand in detail the meaning of what was stated by me in brief. One clinging to form is bound by Māra; one not clinging is freed from the Evil One. One clinging to feeling. . . . One clinging to perception. . . . One clinging to volitional activities. . . . One clinging to consciousness is bound by Māra; one not clinging is freed from the Evil One. It is in such a way that the meaning of what was stated by me in brief should be seen in detail."

Then that monk, having delighted and rejoiced in the Blessed One's statement, rose from his seat, and, after paying homage to the Blessed One, having circumambulated him, departed.

Then, dwelling alone, withdrawn, heedful, ardent, and resolute, that monk, in no long time, by realizing it for himself with direct knowledge, in this present life entered and dwelled in that unsurpassed goal of the spiritual life for the sake of which young people rightly go forth from the household life into homelessness. He directly knew: "Finished is birth, the spiritual life has been lived, what had to be done has been done, there is no further for this state of being." And that monk became one of the arahants.

11. *Rādhasutta*
Rādha (SN 22:71; III 79–80)

Then the Venerable Rādha approached the Blessed One, paid homage to him, and sat down to one side. Seated to one side, the Venerable Rādha said this to the Blessed One: "How, Bhante, does one know, how does one see, so that I-making, mine-making, and tendencies to conceit do not occur in regard to this sentient body and in regard to all external objects?"[26]

"Whatever form there is, Rādha, whether past, future, or present, internal or external, gross or subtle, inferior or superior, far or near—one sees all form as it really is with correct wisdom thus: 'This is not mine, this I am not, this is not my self.' Whatever feeling there is. . . . Whatever perception there is. . . . Whatever volitional activities there are. . . . Whatever consciousness there is, whether past, future, or present, internal or external, gross or subtle, inferior or superior, far or near—one sees all consciousness as it really is with correct wisdom thus: 'This is not mine, this I am not, this is not my self.'

"For one knowing thus, Rādha, for one seeing thus, I-making, mine-making, and tendencies to conceit do not occur in regard to this sentient body and in regard to all external objects.". . . And the Venerable Rādha became one of the arahants.

12. *Sīhasutta*
The Lion (SN 22:78; III 84–86)

"The lion, monks, the king of beasts, comes out from his lair in the evening. Having come out, he stretches, surveys the four directions all around, and roars a lion's roar three times. Having roared a lion's roar three times, he departs for his feeding ground.

"Those animals that hear the roar of the lion, the king of beasts, for the most part acquire fear, a sense of urgency, and terror. Those who live in holes enter holes; those who live in the water enter the water; those who live in the woods enter the woods; the birds resort to the sky. Even the king's bull elephants, bound by strong thongs in the villages, towns, and royal cities, burst and split those bonds; then frightened, discharging urine and feces, they flee here and there. So powerful, monks, is the lion, the king of beasts, over the animals, so commanding, so mighty.

"So too, monks, when the Tathāgata arises in the world, an arahant, perfectly enlightened, accomplished in clear knowledge and conduct, fortunate, knower of the world, unsurpassed trainer of persons to be tamed, teacher of devas and humans, the Enlightened One, the Blessed One, he teaches the Dhamma thus: 'Such is form, such its origin, such its passing away; such is feeling . . . such is perception . . . such are volitional activities . . . such is consciousness, such its origin, such its passing away.'

"Then, monks, even those devas that are long-lived, beautiful, abounding in happiness, dwelling for a long time in tall palaces, when they hear the Tathāgata's Dhamma teaching, for the most part acquire fear, a sense of urgency, and terror,[27] saying: 'It seems, sir, that being actually impermanent, we thought we were permanent. It seems that being actually fleeting, we thought we were lasting. It seems that being actually non-eternal, we thought we were eternal. It seems that we are impermanent, not lasting, non-eternal, included in the personal-assemblage.'[28] So powerful, monks, is the Tathāgata over this world together with its devas, so commanding, so mighty."

This is what the Blessed One said. Having said this, the Fortunate One, the Teacher, further said this:

> When the Buddha, through direct knowledge,
> sets in motion the Wheel of Dhamma,
> the peerless teacher in this world
> with its devas [makes this known]:
>
> The cessation of the personal-assemblage
> and the origin of the personal-assemblage,
> also the noble eightfold path
> that leads to the stilling of suffering.
>
> Then those devas with long lifespans,
> beautiful, ablaze with glory,
> are struck with fear, filled with terror,
> like beasts who hear the lion's roar.

"We've not transcended the personal-assemblage;
it seems, sir, we're impermanent."
[So they say] having heard the utterance
of the arahant, the Stable One released.

13. *Puṇṇamasutta*
Full Moon (SN 22:82; III 100–4)

[1. The request for clarification]
On one occasion the Blessed One was dwelling at Sāvatthī in the Eastern Park, in the mansion of Migāra's mother, together with a great monastic sangha. On that occasion the Blessed One—on that uposatha day, the fifteenth, a full-moon night—was seated out in the open surrounded by the monastic sangha.[29]

Then a certain monk, having risen from his seat, arranged his upper robe over one shoulder, saluted the Blessed One with joined palms, and said this: "Bhante, I would ask the Blessed One about a particular point, if the Blessed One does me the favor of answering my question."

"In that case, monk, sit down in your own seat and ask what you wish."

"Yes, Bhante," that monk replied, sat in his own seat, and said this:

[2. The five aggregates and desire]
"Are these, Bhante, the five clinging-aggregates—that is, the form clinging-aggregate, the feeling clinging-aggregate, the perception clinging-aggregate, the volitional activities clinging-aggregate, the consciousness clinging-aggregate?"

"Those, monk, are the five clinging-aggregates—that is, the form clinging-aggregate . . . the consciousness clinging-aggregate."

Saying, "Good, Bhante," having delighted and rejoiced in the Blessed One's statement, that monk asked a further question: "But, Bhante, in what are these five clinging-aggregates rooted?"

"These five clinging-aggregates, monk, are rooted in desire."[30]

Saying, "Good, Bhante," . . . that monk asked a further question: "Bhante, is that clinging itself [the same as] those five clinging-aggregates or is there clinging apart from the five clinging-aggregates?"

"Monk, that clinging itself is not [the same as] those five clinging-aggregates, nor is there clinging apart from the five clinging-aggregates. But rather the desire-and-lust there [in relation to them], that is the clinging there."[31]

Saying, "Good, Bhante," that monk asked a further question: "Bhante, could there be diversity in the desire-and-lust for the five clinging-aggregates?"

"There could be, monk," the Blessed One said. "Here, monk, it occurs to someone: 'May I have such form in the future, may I have such feeling in the future, may I have such perception in the future, may I have such volitional activities in the future, may I have such consciousness in the future!' Thus, monk, there can be diversity in the desire-and-lust for the five clinging-aggregates."

[3. Designating and describing the aggregates]

Saying, "Good, Bhante," that monk asked a further question: "In what way, Bhante, does the designation 'aggregates' apply to the aggregates?"

"Whatever form there is, monk, whether past, future, or present, internal or external, gross or subtle, inferior or superior, far or near: this is called the 'form aggregate.' Whatever feeling there is, whether past, future, or present . . . this is called the 'feeling aggregate.' Whatever perception there is, whether past, future, or present . . . this is called the 'perception aggregate.' Whatever volitional activities there are, whether past, future, or present . . . these are called the 'volitional-activities aggregate.' Whatever consciousness there is, whether past, future, or present, internal or external, gross or subtle, inferior or superior, far or near: this is called the 'consciousness aggregate.' It is in this way, monk, that the designation 'aggregates' applies to the aggregates."

Saying, "Good, Bhante," that monk asked a further question: "What is the cause and condition, Bhante, for the making known of the form aggregate? What is the cause and condition for the making known of the feeling aggregate? What is the cause and condition for the making known of the perception aggregate? What is the cause and condition for the making known of the volitional-activities aggregate? What is the cause and condition for the making known of the consciousness aggregate?"

"The four great elements, monk, are the cause and condition for the making known of the form aggregate. Contact is the cause and condition for the making known of the feeling aggregate. Contact is the cause and condition for the making known of the perception aggregate. Contact is the cause and condition for the making known of the volitional-activities aggregate. Name-and-form is the cause and condition for the making known of the consciousness aggregate."

[4. The view of the personal-assemblage]

Saying, "Good, Bhante," that monk asked a further question: "How, Bhante, does the view of the personal-assemblage occur?"

"Here, monk, an unlearned worldling, who is not a seer of noble ones, who is unskilled in the noble ones' Dhamma, who is untrained in the noble ones' Dhamma, who is not a seer of good persons, who is unskilled in the good persons' Dhamma, who is untrained in the good persons' Dhamma, regards form as self, or self as possessing form, or form as in self, or self as in form. He regards feeling as self. . . . He regards perception as self. . . . He regards volitional activities as self. . . . He regards consciousness as self, or self as possessing consciousness, or consciousness as in self, or self as in consciousness. That is how the view of the personal-assemblage occurs."

"But, Bhante, how does the view of the personal-assemblage not occur?"

"Here, monk, an instructed noble disciple, who is a seer of the noble ones, who is skilled in the noble ones' Dhamma, who is trained in the noble ones' Dhamma, who is a seer of good persons, who is skilled in the good persons' Dhamma, who is trained in the good persons' Dhamma, does not regard form as self, or self as possessing form, or form as in self, or self as in form. He does not regard feeling as self. . . . He does not regard perception as self. . . . He does not regard volitional activities as self. . . . He does not regard consciousness as self, or self as possessing consciousness, or consciousness as in self, or self as in consciousness. That is how the view of the personal-assemblage does not occur."

[The remaining sections of this sutta open with questions whose answers correspond to 2.5, 2.11, and 2.9.3.]

14. *Pupphasutta*
Flowers (SN 22:94; III 138–40)

[1. Not disputing with the world]
"Monks, I do not dispute with the world; the world, indeed, disputes with me. A speaker of the Dhamma does not dispute with anyone in the world. That which the wise in the world have agreed upon as not existing, I too say of that: 'It does not exist.' That which the wise in the world have agreed upon as existing, I too say of that: 'It exists.'

"And what is it, monks, that the wise in the world have agreed upon as not existing, of which I too say: 'It does not exist'? Form that is permanent, lasting, eternal, not subject to change: the wise in the world have agreed upon this as not existing, and I too say of that: 'It does not exist.' Feeling that is permanent. . . . Perception that is permanent. . . . Volitional activities that are permanent. . . . Consciousness that is permanent, lasting, eternal, not subject to change: the wise in the world have agreed upon this as not existing, and I too say of that: 'It does not exist.' This is what the wise in the world have agreed upon as not existing, of which I too say: 'It does not exist.'

"And what is it, monks, that the wise in the world have agreed upon as existing, of which I too say: 'It exists'? Form that is impermanent, suffering, subject to change: the wise in the world have agreed upon this as existing, and I too say of that: 'It exists.' Feeling that is impermanent. . . . Perception that is impermanent. . . . Volitional activities that are impermanent. . . . Consciousness that is impermanent, suffering, subject to change: the wise in the world have agreed upon this as existing, and I too say of that: 'It exists.' This is what the wise in the world have agreed upon as existing, of which I too say: 'It exists.'

[2. World phenomena in the world]
"There is, monks, a world-phenomenon in the world about which the Tathāgata has become enlightened and made the breakthrough. Having become enlightened to it and made the

breakthrough to it, he points it out, teaches it, makes it known, establishes it, discloses it, analyzes it, and elucidates it.

"And what is that world-phenomenon in the world about which the Tathāgata has become enlightened and made the breakthrough, and which he then points out, teaches, makes known, establishes, discloses, analyzes, and elucidates? Form, monks, is a world-phenomenon in the world about which the Tathāgata has become enlightened and made the breakthrough, and which he then points out, teaches, makes known, establishes, discloses, analyzes, and elucidates.

"When it is being thus pointed out, taught, made known, established, disclosed, analyzed, and elucidated by the Tathāgata, if anyone does not know and see, how can I do anything with that foolish worldling who is blind and sightless, who does not know and does not see?

"Feeling is a world-phenomenon in the world. . . . Perception is a world-phenomenon in the world. . . . Volitional activities are a world-phenomenon in the world. . . . Consciousness is a world-phenomenon in the world about which the Tathāgata has become enlightened and made the breakthrough, and which he then points out, teaches, makes known, establishes, discloses, analyzes, and elucidates.

"When it is being thus pointed out, taught, made known, established, disclosed, analyzed, and elucidated by the Tathāgata, if anyone does not know and see, how can I do anything with that foolish worldling who is blind and sightless, who does not know and does not see?

[3. The simile of the lotus]

"Monks, just as a blue, red, or white lotus is born in the water and grows up in the water, but having risen from the water, it stands untainted by the water, so too the Tathāgata was born in the world and grew up in the world, but having overcome the world, he dwells untainted by the world."

15. *Pheṇapiṇḍūpamasutta*

Simile of the Lump of Foam (SN 22:95; III 140–42)

[1. Form]

On one occasion the Blessed One was dwelling at Ayojjhā on

the bank of the Ganges River. There the Blessed One addressed the monks: "Suppose, monks, this Ganges River would carry along a great lump of foam. A clear-sighted man would see it, ponder it, and thoroughly investigate it. As he does so, it would appear to him to be void, it would appear hollow, it would appear insubstantial. For what substance could there be in a lump of foam?

"So too, monks, whatever form there is, whether past, future, or present, internal or external, gross or subtle, inferior or superior, far or near: a monk sees it, ponders it, and thoroughly investigates it. As he does so, it appears to him to be void, it appears hollow, it appears insubstantial. For what substance could there be in form?[32]

[2. Feeling]

"Suppose, monks, in the autumn, when the sky is raining with big raindrops falling, a water bubble arises and ceases on the water's surface. A clear-sighted man would see this, ponder it, and thoroughly investigate it. As he does so, it would appear to him to be void, it would appear hollow, it would appear insubstantial. For what substance could there be in a water bubble?

"So too, monks, whatever feeling there is, whether past, future, or present, internal or external, gross or subtle, inferior or superior, far or near: a monk sees it, ponders it, and thoroughly investigates it. As he does so, it appears to him to be void, it appears hollow, it appears insubstantial. For what substance could there be in feeling?[33]

[3. Perception]

"Suppose, monks, in the last month of the hot season, at midday, a mirage shimmers. A clear-sighted man would see this, ponder it, and thoroughly investigate it. As he does so, it would appear to him to be void, it would appear hollow, it would appear insubstantial. For what substance could there be in a mirage?

"So too, monks, whatever perception there is, whether past, future, or present, internal or external, gross or subtle, inferior or superior, far or near: a monk sees it, ponders it, and thoroughly investigates it. As he does so, it appears to him to be void, it appears hollow, it appears insubstantial. For what substance could there be in perception?[34]

[4. Volitional activities]
"Suppose, monks, a man needing heartwood, seeking heartwood, wandering on a search for heartwood, would take a sharp axe and enter a woods. There he would see a large plantain trunk, straight, fresh, without an inflorescence. He would cut it down at the root, cut it off at the crown, and unroll the coil. As he unrolls the coil, he would not find even softwood; how then heartwood? A clear-sighted man would see this, ponder it, and thoroughly investigate it. As he does so, it would appear to him to be void, it would appear hollow, it would appear insubstantial. For what substance could there be in a plantain trunk?

"So too, monks, whatever volitional activities there are, whether past, future, or present, internal or external, gross or subtle, inferior or superior, far or near: a monk sees them, ponders them, and thoroughly investigates them. As he does so, they appear to him to be void, they appear hollow, they appear insubstantial. For what substance could there be in volitional activities?[35]

[5. Consciousness]
"Suppose, monks, a magician or a magician's apprentice were to display a magical illusion at a crossroads. A clear-sighted man would see this, ponder it, and thoroughly investigate it. As he does so, it would appear to him to be void, it would appear hollow, it would appear insubstantial. For what substance could there be in a magical illusion?

"So too, monks, whatever consciousness there is, whether past, future, or present, internal or external, gross or subtle, inferior or superior, far or near: a monk sees it, ponders it, and thoroughly investigates it. As he does so, it appears to him to be void, it appears hollow, it appears insubstantial. For what substance could there be in consciousness?[36]

[6. Liberation]
"Thus seeing, monks, the learned noble disciple becomes disenchanted with form, disenchanted with feeling, disenchanted with perception, disenchanted with volitional activities, disenchanted with consciousness. Being disenchanted, he becomes dispassionate. Through dispassion he is liberated. In regard to what is liberated, the knowledge occurs thus: 'Liberated.' He

understands: 'Finished is birth, the spiritual life has been lived, what had to be done has been done, there is no further for this state of being.'"

This is what the Blessed One said. Having said this, the Fortunate One, the Teacher, further said this:

Form is like a lump of foam,
feeling like a water bubble;
perception is like a mirage,
volitions like a plantain trunk,
and consciousness like an illusion:
so explained the Kinsman of the Sun.[37]

However one may ponder it
and thoroughly investigate it,
it appears but hollow and void
when one views it carefully.

With reference to this body
the One of Broad Wisdom has taught
that with the abandoning of three things
one sees this form discarded.

When vitality, heat, and consciousness
depart from this physical body,
then it lies there cast away:
food for others, without volition.

Such is this continuum,
this illusion, beguiler of fools.
It is taught to be a murderer;
here no substance can be found.

A monk with energy aroused
should look upon the aggregates thus,
whether by day or at night,
comprehending, ever mindful.

He should discard all the fetters
and make a refuge for himself.

Let him practice as with head ablaze,
aspiring for the imperishable state.

16. *Aniccasaññāsutta*
Perception of the Impermanent (SN 22:102; III 155–57)

"Perception of the impermanent, monks, developed and cultivated, eliminates all sensual lust, eliminates all lust for form, eliminates all lust for existence, eliminates all ignorance, demolishes all conceit 'I am.'

"Just as, monks, in the autumn a plowman, plowing with a great plow, splits apart all root filaments as he plows, just so, perception of the impermanent, developed and cultivated, eliminates all sensual lust, eliminates all lust for form, eliminates all lust for existence, eliminates all ignorance, demolishes all conceit 'I am.' . . .

"Just as, monks, whatever radiance there is of the stars, all that is not worth a sixteenth portion of the radiance of the moon, [such that] the radiance of the moon is declared chief among them, just so, perception of the impermanent . . . demolishes all conceit 'I am.'

"Just as, monks, in autumn, when the sky is clear, rid of clouds, the sun, rising through the firmament, disperses all darkness throughout space and shines and beams and radiates, just so, perception of the impermanent, developed and cultivated, eliminates all sensual lust, eliminates all lust for form, eliminates all lust for existence, eliminates all ignorance, demolishes all conceit 'I am.'

"And how, monks, is perception of the impermanent developed, how is it cultivated, so that it eliminates all sensual lust . . . demolishes all conceit 'I am'? 'Such is form, such its origin, such its passing away; such is feeling . . . such is perception . . . such are volitional activities . . . such is consciousness, such its origin, such its passing away.' When, monks, perception of the impermanent is thus developed, thus cultivated, it eliminates all sensual lust, eliminates all lust for form, eliminates all lust for existence, eliminates all ignorance, demolishes all conceit 'I am.'"

3. The Six Sense Bases: The Channels through Which Suffering Originates

Introduction

The six sense bases, treated in detail in chapter 35 of the Saṃyutta Nikāya, are another structure, complementary to the five aggregates, that the Buddha uses to explore the nature of experience and thus to uncover the nature of dukkha. The sense bases occur in pairs, internal and external. The six internal sense bases are the sensory faculties through which the mind gains access to sense objects and thereby to the world. Since all conditioned experience is included in the noble truth of suffering, the six internal bases may be called "the channels through which suffering originates." A discourse in the Saccasaṃyutta (SN 56:14, at V 426), in fact, concisely defines the noble truth of suffering as the six internal sense bases.

The six internal bases each have a corresponding external base, making twelve bases in all: the eye and visible forms, the ear and sounds, the nose and odors, the tongue and tastes, the body and tactile objects, and the mind and mental objects. The pairs are called "bases" (*āyatana*) because each serves as the platform for the arising of the corresponding type of consciousness. Thus eye-consciousness arises in dependence on the eye and visible forms, ear-consciousness in dependence on the ear and sounds, and each of the other types of consciousness in dependence on its respective internal and external bases. From this it can be seen that the principle of conditionality, which underlies the formula of dependent origination (explored in the following chapter), also governs the arising of consciousness, undercutting the notion of consciousness as a stable, autonomous subject of experience.

The exact referent of the mind-base (*manāyatana*) is ambiguous. The Abhidhamma identifies the mind-base with consciousness in its entirety, and thus with all six classes of consciousness.[38] However, since the mind (*mano*) is repeatedly said to be the base for the arising of mind-consciousness, it seems unlikely that this interpretation conveys the original intention of the suttas, which treat the mind-base as analogous to the other sense bases in relation to their corresponding types of consciousness. There is no indication, though, that the mind-base is material; rather, it seems to be an internal mental organ. If we treat the two immaterial bases as parallel to the material internal and external bases, we might understand the mind-base to be the support for the arising of mind-consciousness (*manoviññāṇa*), and the base of mental objects (*dhammāyatana*) to be the objective sphere of mind-consciousness. On this interpretation, the mind-base might be taken as the passive subliminal flow of mind from which active reflective consciousness emerges, and its corresponding external base to be the purely mental objects apprehended by acts of thought, introspection, imagination, reflection, and meditative contemplation.

Internal sense bases	*External sense bases*	*Types of consciousness arisen from the sense bases*
eye	forms	eye-consciousness
ear	sounds	ear-consciousness
nose	smells	nose-consciousness
tongue	tastes	tongue-consciousness
body	tactile objects	body-consciousness
mind	mental objects	mind-consciousness

Whereas the scheme of the five aggregates seems to have been advanced primarily to show the objective ground for the deluded notions of "mine," "I," and "self," the six sense bases have a closer connection with craving. This point is underscored by the classical formula for dependent origination, within which we find the sequence: the six sense bases > contact > feeling > craving. The meeting of the sense base, object, and consciousness is called "contact" (*phassa*), and since they mediate between consciousness and its objects, the internal sense bases are also called the "bases for contact" (*phassāyatana*). With contact as condition there arises feeling (see **3.4**), and this in turn conditions craving.

Since craving is the origin of dukkha, and craving is nurtured by the feelings originating through contact at the six sense bases, to eliminate craving we must change our perspective on sense objects and the feelings they provoke. The task of regulating craving—and other unwholesome responses to feeling—requires us to control our reactions to the input of the senses. To facilitate this, a practice called "restraint of the senses" (*indriyasaṃvara*) is inserted into the sequential training of the disciple, where it serves as a bridge between ethical behavior and formal meditation. The practice is described by a stock formula that runs thus:

> On seeing a form with the eye, the monk does not grasp at its signs and features. Since, if he left the eye faculty unguarded, evil unwholesome states of longing and dejection might invade him, he practices the way of its restraint, he guards the eye faculty, he undertakes the restraint of the eye faculty. On hearing a sound with the ear. . . . On smelling an odor with the nose. . . . On tasting a flavor with the tongue. . . . On touching a tactile object with the body. . . . On cognizing a mental object with the mind, he does not grasp at its signs and features. Since, if he left the mind faculty unguarded, evil unwholesome states of longing and dejection might invade him, he practices the way of its restraint, he guards the mind faculty, he undertakes the restraint of the mind faculty.[39]

Together with moderation in eating and devotion to wakefulness, restraint of the senses is said to constitute the foundation for the destruction of the influxes.[40]

Especially critical, in the above passage, is the injunction not to grasp at the signs and features of the object.[41] It is when we grasp at these signs and features—the object's attractive and repulsive aspects—that we begin mentally proliferating the bare input of sense data in ways that provoke our desires and thereby entangle us more tightly in the web of craving and aversion. Instead of responding to feelings instinctively, relishing pleasant feelings and resisting painful feelings, the Buddha instructs us to see how feeling is merely a conditioned state that arises through a complex process involving the sense bases, consciousness, and contact.

On some occasions, simply discerning the conditioned origin of feeling is sufficient to short-circuit the entire cascade of events by which feeling overwhelms the mind. Instead of letting the mind run out to the object, one redirects the beam of attention to the process by which the experience is generated, exposing its constructed nature and the intrinsic impermanence of all the factors entering into the process. As **3.4** states, seeing how feeling arises on the basis of sensory contact, "one becomes disenchanted with the eye, disenchanted with forms, disenchanted with eye-consciousness, disenchanted with eye-contact, disenchanted with whatever feeling arises with eye-contact as condition."

Feeling can be either pleasant, painful, or neutral—that is, neither painful nor pleasant. Each of these feelings is correlated with one of the three root defilements. Pleasant feeling is the trigger for lust, painful feeling for hatred, and neutral feeling for delusion. As long as lust, hatred, and delusion consume the mind, the entire field of sense experience, right down to the internal and external sense bases, blazes with the fires of lust, hatred, and delusion and with the fires of birth, old age, and death. This is the theme of the famous "Fire Sermon" (**3.2**), which begins with the startling proclamation that "everything is burning," burning with the fires of the defilements and the suffering of repeated birth, aging, and death.

Where the suttas on the five aggregates emphasize the absence of a self among the aggregates, and thus stress the contemplation of non-self, the suttas on the six sense bases emphasize the contemplation of impermanence. Of course, this is a matter of emphasis, and both contemplations apply to both sets of factors. But it seems that the analysis into the five aggregates is designed to expose the composite nature of experience and thereby overturn the view of a self, which is merely one of the lower fetters eliminated at the first stage of realization, known as stream-entry. In contrast, craving, being the driving force of saṃsāra, is removed only with the attainment of arahantship, the final stage of realization; thus the direct assault on craving marks a higher stage of the path.

Craving springs up and thrives because we take enjoyable feelings to be permanent and thus tacitly assume we can go on enjoying them forever. When seen rightly, however, all the constituents of sensory experience turn out to be fleeting and impermanent. The internal sense bases, their objects, the corresponding types of consciousness, and the contacts between them must be seen as "impermanent, changing, and becoming otherwise" (**3.7**). The same is true for the feeling, perception, and volition that arise through contact. When one directly sees the impermanence of feelings, the associated contacts, and the sense bases through which those contacts originate, ignorance is abandoned and clear knowledge arises (**3.3**).

Each of the sense faculties is naturally drawn to its corresponding object. Normally, we rejoice when we gain the objects of desire, but in doing so we set ourselves up for a fall; for when those objects cease and perish, our delight vanishes and we plunge into dejection and anguish. Delight in sense objects obstructs the path to nibbāna, the final goal of the spiritual life; by dispelling delight one dwells happily and attains nibbāna (**3.8**). Agreeable sense objects are compared to a fisherman's bait, and Māra, the Evil One, is like a fisherman. The sense objects are "six hooks for the misery of beings." Those who delight in these objects have "swallowed the bait of Māra" and come under his control, while those who do not delight in them escape Māra's control (**3.11**).

The bondage created by the six pairs of sense bases does not lie in the sense bases themselves but in the craving that arises through their interaction. Text **3.12** tells us that just as, when a black ox and a white ox are yoked together by a single harness, what binds them together is the harness, so the eye is not the fetter of forms nor forms the fetter of the eye, but the desire-and-lust that arises in dependence on them is the fetter. The Buddha himself has eyes and sees forms with his eyes, but he has eradicated craving and is thereby liberated in mind. This sets the task for the disciple as well. The purpose of the training is to remove craving and thereby win liberation of mind.

The six senses are compared to six kinds of animals (**3.15**). When bound together and then released, each animal rushes toward its familiar habitat. In the same way, without the exercise of restraint and self-control, each of the senses will instinctively run toward its respective object. But if the animals are tied to a firm post or pillar, though they pull in different directions, eventually they become fatigued, settle down, and become still. Similarly, when the senses are tied to a strong pillar, they too will settle down and become still. That pillar, the Buddha says, is mindfulness of the body.

1. *Pahānasutta*
Abandoning (SN 35:24; IV 15–16)

"I will teach you, monks, the Dhamma for abandoning all. Listen to that. And what, monks, is the Dhamma for abandoning all? The eye is to be abandoned, forms are to be abandoned, eye-consciousness is to be abandoned, eye-contact is to be abandoned, and whatever feeling arises with eye-contact as condition—whether pleasant or painful or neither-painful-nor-pleasant—that too is to be abandoned.

"The ear is to be abandoned. . . . The nose is to be abandoned. . . . The tongue is to be abandoned. . . . The body is to be abandoned. . . . The mind is to be abandoned, mental objects are to be abandoned, mind-consciousness is to be abandoned, mind-contact is to be abandoned, and whatever feeling arises with mind-contact as condition—whether pleasant or painful or neither-painful-nor-pleasant—that too is to be abandoned. This is the Dhamma for abandoning all."

2. *Ādittasutta*
Burning (SN 35:28; IV 19–20)

On one occasion the Blessed One was dwelling at Gayā, at Gayā's Head, together with a thousand monks.[42] There the Blessed One addressed the monks: "Monks, all is burning. And what, monks, is the all that is burning? The eye is burning, forms are burning, eye-consciousness is burning, eye-contact is burning, and whatever feeling arises with eye-contact as condition—

whether pleasant or painful or neither-painful-nor-pleasant—that too is burning.

"Burning with what? 'Burning with the fire of lust, with the fire of hatred, with the fire of delusion; burning with birth, old age, and death; with sorrow, lamentation, pain, dejection, and misery,' I say. . . .

"The ear is burning. . . . The nose is burning. . . . The tongue is burning. . . . The body is burning. . . . The mind is burning, mental objects are burning, mind-consciousness is burning, mind-contact is burning, and whatever feeling arises with mind-contact as condition—whether pleasant or painful or neither-painful-nor-pleasant—that too is burning. Burning with what? 'Burning with the fire of lust, with the fire of hatred, with the fire of delusion; burning with birth, old age, and death; with sorrow, lamentation, pain, dejection, and misery,' I say.

"Seeing thus, monks, the learned noble disciple becomes disenchanted with the eye, disenchanted with forms, disenchanted with eye-consciousness, disenchanted with eye-contact, disenchanted with whatever feeling arises with eye-contact as condition—whether pleasant or painful or neither-painful-nor-pleasant. . . . He becomes disenchanted with the mind, disenchanted with mental objects, disenchanted with mind-consciousness, disenchanted with mind-contact, disenchanted with whatever feeling arises with mind-contact as condition—whether pleasant or painful or neither-painful-nor-pleasant.

"Being disenchanted, he becomes dispassionate. Through dispassion he is liberated. In regard to what is liberated, the knowledge occurs thus: 'Liberated.' He understands: 'Finished is birth, the spiritual life has been lived, what had to be done has been done, there is no further for this state of being.'"

This is what the Blessed One said. Elated, those monks delighted in the Blessed One's statement. And while this discourse was being spoken, through non-clinging the minds of the thousand monks were liberated from the influxes.

5. *Avijjāpahānasutta*
Abandoning Ignorance (SN 35:53; IV 30–31)

Then a certain monk approached the Blessed One, paid homage to him, and sat down to one side. Seated to one side, that monk said this to the Blessed One: "How, Bhante, does one know, how does one see, so that ignorance is abandoned and clear knowledge arises?"

"For one knowing and seeing the eye as impermanent, monk, ignorance is abandoned and clear knowledge arises. For one knowing and seeing forms as impermanent, ignorance is abandoned and clear knowledge arises. For one knowing and seeing eye-consciousness as impermanent, ignorance is abandoned and clear knowledge arises. For one knowing and seeing eye-contact as impermanent, ignorance is abandoned and clear knowledge arises. For one knowing and seeing as impermanent whatever feeling arises with eye-contact as condition—whether pleasant or painful or neither-painful-nor-pleasant—ignorance is abandoned and clear knowledge arises. . . .

"For one knowing and seeing the mind as impermanent, ignorance is abandoned and clear knowledge arises. For one knowing and seeing mental objects as impermanent, ignorance is abandoned and clear knowledge arises. For one knowing and seeing mind-consciousness as impermanent, ignorance is abandoned and clear knowledge arises. For one knowing and seeing mind-contact as impermanent, ignorance is abandoned and clear knowledge arises. For one knowing and seeing as impermanent whatever feeling arises with mind-contact as condition—whether pleasant or painful or neither-painful-nor-pleasant—ignorance is abandoned and clear knowledge arises. For one knowing thus, for one seeing thus, ignorance is abandoned and clear knowledge arises."

4. *Sabbupādānapariññāsutta*
Full Understanding of All Clinging (SN 35:60; IV 32–33)

"I will teach you, monks, the Dhamma for the full understanding of all clinging. Listen to that. And what, monks, is the Dhamma for the full understanding of all clinging? In dependence on the eye and forms, eye-consciousness arises. The meeting of the three is contact. With contact as condition, feeling [comes to be]. Seeing thus, the learned noble disciple becomes disenchanted with the eye, disenchanted with forms, disenchanted with eye-consciousness, disenchanted with eye-contact, disenchanted with feeling. Being disenchanted, he becomes dispassionate. Through dispassion [the mind] is liberated. Through emancipation he understands: 'Clinging has been fully understood by me.' . . .

"In dependence on the mind and mental objects, mind-consciousness arises. The meeting of the three is contact. With contact as condition, feeling [comes to be]. Seeing thus, the learned noble disciple becomes disenchanted with the mind, disenchanted with mental objects, disenchanted with mind-consciousness, disenchanted with mind-contact, disenchanted with feeling. Being disenchanted, he becomes dispassionate. Through dispassion [the mind] is liberated. Through emancipation he understands: 'Clinging has been fully understood by me.' This, monks, is the Dhamma for the full understanding of all clinging."

5. *Upavāṇasutta*
Upavāṇa (SN 35:70; IV 41–43)

[1. When lust is present]
Then the Venerable Upavāṇa approached the Blessed One . . . and said this to the Blessed One: "It is said, Bhante, 'a directly visible Dhamma, a directly visible Dhamma.' In what way, Bhante, is the Dhamma directly visible, immediate, asking one to come and see, applicable, to be personally understood by the wise?"

"Here, Upavāṇa, having seen a form with the eye, a monk experiences the form and experiences lust for the form, and he understands the lust for forms existing internally thus, 'There exists for me internally lust for forms.' Since, Upavāṇa, having seen that form with the eye, the monk experiences the form and experiences lust for the form, and he understands the lust for forms existing internally thus, 'There exists for me internally lust for forms,' in such a way the Dhamma is directly visible, immediate, asking one to come and see, applicable, to be personally understood by the wise. . . .

"Again, Upavāṇa, having cognized a mental object with the mind, a monk experiences the mental object and experiences lust for the mental object, and he understands the lust for mental objects existing internally thus, 'There exists for me internally lust for mental objects.' Since, Upavāṇa, having cognized that mental object with the mind, a monk experiences the mental object and experiences lust for the mental object, and he understands the lust for mental objects existing internally thus, 'There exists for me internally lust for mental objects,' in such a way, too, the Dhamma is directly visible, immediate, asking one to come and see, applicable, to be personally understood by the wise.

[2. When lust is absent]
"But here, Upavāṇa, having seen a form with the eye, a monk experiences the form but does not experience lust for the form, and he understands there is no lust for forms existing internally thus, 'There does not exist for me internally lust for forms.' Since, Upavāṇa, having seen that form with the eye, the monk experiences the form but does not experience lust for the form, and he understands there is no lust for forms existing internally thus, 'There does not exist for me internally lust for forms,' in such a way, too, the Dhamma is directly visible, immediate, asking one to come and see, applicable, to be personally understood by the wise. . . .

"Again, Upavāṇa, having cognized a mental object with the mind, a monk experiences the mental object but does not experience lust for the mental object, and he understands there is no lust for mental objects existing internally thus, 'There does not exist for me internally lust for mental objects.' Since, Upavāṇa, having cognized that mental object with the mind, the monk experiences the mental object but does not experience lust for the mental object, and he understands there is no lust for mental objects existing internally thus, 'There does not exist for me internally lust for mental objects,' in such a way, too, the Dhamma is directly visible, immediate, asking one to come and see, applicable, to be personally understood by the wise."

6. *Suññalokasutta*
Empty World (SN 35:85; IV 54)

Then the Venerable Ānanda approached the Blessed One . . . and said this to the Blessed One: "It is said, Bhante: 'The world is empty, the world is empty.' In what way, Bhante, is it said: 'The world is empty'?"

"Because, Ānanda, it is empty of self and of what belongs to self, it is therefore said: 'The world is empty.' And what, Ānanda, is empty of self and of what belongs to self? The eye is empty of self and of what belongs to self. Forms are empty of self and of what belongs to self. Eye-consciousness is empty of self and of what belongs to self. Eye-contact is empty of self and of what belongs to self. Whatever feeling arises with eye-contact as condition—whether pleasant or painful or neither-painful-nor-pleasant—that too is empty of self and of what belongs to self.

"The ear is empty. . . . The nose is empty. . . . The tongue is empty. . . . The body is empty. . . . The mind is empty of self and of what belongs to self. Mental objects are empty of self and of what belongs to self. Mind-consciousness is empty of self and of what belongs to self. Mind-contact is empty of self and of what belongs to self. Whatever feeling arises with mind-contact as condition—whether pleasant or painful or neither-painful-nor-pleasant—that too is empty of self and of what belongs to self. Because, Ānanda, it is empty of self and of what belongs to self, it is therefore said: 'The world is empty.'"

7. *Dvayasutta*
Dyads (SN 35:93; IV 67–69)

"Consciousness, monks, comes to be in dependence on a dyad. And how, monks, does consciousness come to be in dependence on a dyad?

"In dependence on the eye and forms, eye-consciousness arises. The eye is impermanent, changing, becoming otherwise. Forms are impermanent, changing, becoming otherwise. Thus this dyad is moving and tottering, impermanent, changing, becoming otherwise.

"Eye-consciousness is impermanent, changing, becoming otherwise. The cause and condition for the arising of eye-consciousness too is impermanent, changing, becoming otherwise. When eye-consciousness has arisen in dependence on an impermanent condition, how could it be permanent?

"The meeting, the encounter, the concurrence of these three

things is called 'eye-contact.' Eye-contact too is impermanent, changing, becoming otherwise. The cause and condition for the arising of eye-contact too is impermanent, changing, becoming otherwise. When, monks, eye-contact has arisen in dependence on a condition that is impermanent, how could it be permanent?

"Contacted, monks, one feels, contacted one wills, contacted one perceives. Thus these things too are moving and tottering, impermanent, changing, becoming otherwise. . . .

"In dependence on the mind and mental objects, mind-consciousness arises. The mind is impermanent, changing, becoming otherwise. Mental objects are impermanent, changing, becoming otherwise. . . . Contacted, monks, one feels, contacted one wills, contacted one perceives. Thus these things too are moving and tottering, impermanent, changing, becoming otherwise. In such a way, monks, consciousness comes to be in dependence on a dyad."

8. *Sakkapañhasutta*
Sakka's Questions (SN 35:118; IV 101–2)

[1. Why beings do not attain nibbāna]
On one occasion the Blessed One was dwelling at Rājagaha on Vulture Peak Mountain. Then Sakka, lord of the devas,[43] approached the Blessed One, paid homage to him, stood to one side, and said this to the Blessed One:

"Bhante, what is the cause, what is the reason, why some beings here do not attain nibbāna in this present life? And what is the cause, what is the reason, why some beings here attain nibbāna in this present life?"

"There are, lord of the devas, forms cognizable by the eye that are wished for, desired, agreeable, of a pleasing nature, connected with sensuality, enticing. If a monk delights in them, welcomes them, and remains holding them, as he does so, his consciousness becomes dependent on them and stands clinging to them. A monk with clinging does not attain nibbāna. . . .

"There are, lord of the devas, mental objects cognizable by the mind that are wished for, desired, agreeable, of a pleasing nature, connected with sensuality, enticing. If a monk delights in them, welcomes them, and remains holding to them, as he does so, his consciousness becomes dependent on them and stands clinging to them. A monk with clinging does not attain nibbāna. This is the cause, this is the reason, why some beings here do not attain nibbāna in this present life.

[2. How beings attain nibbāna]
"There are, lord of the devas, forms cognizable by the eye that are wished for, desired, agreeable, of a pleasing nature, connected with sensuality, enticing. If a monk does not delight in them, does not welcome them, and does not remain holding to them, as he does so, his consciousness does not become dependent on them and stand clinging to them. A monk without clinging attains nibbāna.

"There are, lord of the devas, mental objects cognizable by the mind that are wished for, desired, agreeable, of a pleasing nature, connected with sensuality, enticing. If a monk does not delight in them, does not welcome them, and does not remain holding to them, as he does so, his consciousness does not become dependent on them and stand clinging to them. . . . A monk without clinging attains nibbāna. This is the cause, this is the reason, why some beings here attain nibbāna in this present life."

9. *Rūpārāmasutta*
Delight in Forms (SN 35:136; IV 126–28)

"Monks, devas and humans delight in forms, are delighted with forms, rejoice in forms. With the change, fading away, and cessation of forms, devas and humans dwell painfully. Devas and humans delight in sounds . . . delight in odors . . . delight in tastes . . . delight in tactile objects . . . delight in mental objects, are delighted with mental objects, rejoice in mental objects. With the change, fading away, and cessation of mental objects, devas and humans dwell painfully.

"But, monks, the Tathāgata, the arahant, the perfectly enlightened one, having known as they really are the origin and the passing away, the enjoyment, the danger, and the escape in the case of forms, does not delight in forms, is not delighted with forms, does not rejoice in forms. With the change, fading away, and cessation of forms, the Tathāgata dwells happily.

Having known as they really are the origin and the passing away, the enjoyment, the danger, and the escape in the case of sounds . . . in the case of odors . . . in the case of tastes . . . in the case of tactile objects . . . in the case of mental objects, the Tathāgata does not delight in mental objects, is not delighted with mental objects, does not rejoice in mental objects. With the change, fading away, and cessation of mental objects, the Tathāgata dwells happily."

This is what the Blessed One said. Having said this, the Fortunate One, the Teacher, further said this:

Forms, sounds, odors, tastes,
tactile objects, and all mental objects—
they are desirable, lovely, and agreeable
so long as they continue to exist.

These are considered happiness
by the world with its devas;
but where these cease,
that they consider suffering.

The noble ones have seen as happiness
the ceasing of the personal-assemblage.
This [view] of those who clearly see
runs counter to the entire world.

What others speak of as happiness,
that the noble ones say is suffering;
what others speak of as suffering,
that the noble ones know as bliss.

Behold this Dhamma hard to comprehend:
here the foolish are bewildered.
For those with blocked minds it is obscure,
sheer darkness for those who do not see.

But for the good it is disclosed;
it is light here for those who see.
The dullards unskilled in the Dhamma
don't understand it in its presence.

This Dhamma isn't easily understood
by those afflicted with lust for existence,
who flow along in the stream of existence,
deeply mired in Māra's realm.

Who else apart from the noble ones
are able to understand this state?
When they have rightly known that state,
the taintless ones are fully quenched.

10. *Samuddasutta*
The Ocean (SN 35:228 [187]; IV 157)

"'The ocean, the ocean,' monks, the unlearned worldling says. This, monks, is not the ocean in the discipline of the noble one. This is a great mass of water, a great flood of water.

"The eye, monks, is a person's ocean, its current consisting of forms. One who endures that current consisting of forms is called '[one who has] crossed the ocean of the eye with its waves, with its whirlpools, with its sharks, with its demons.' Crossed, gone beyond, the brahmin stands on high ground. . . .

"The mind, monks, is a person's ocean, its current consisting of mental objects. One who endures that current consisting of mental objects is called '[one who has] crossed the ocean of the mind with its waves, with its whirlpools, with its sharks, with its demons.' Crossed, gone beyond, the brahmin stands on high ground."

This is what the Blessed One said. Having said this, the Fortunate One, the Teacher, further said this:

One who has crossed this ocean so hard to cross,
with its dangers of sharks, demons, and waves,
the knowledge-master who has lived the spiritual life,
reached the world's end, is called "one gone beyond."

11. *Bālisikopamasutta*
Simile of the Fisherman (SN 35:230 [189]; IV 158–59)

"Suppose, monks, a fisherman would throw a baited hook into a pool of deep water. A certain fish with an eye for bait would swallow it. Thus the fish that has swallowed the fisherman's hook has incurred misery, has incurred disaster, is to be done with by the fisherman as he desires.

"Just so, monks, these six hooks in the world are for the misery of beings, for the harm of living beings. What six? There are, monks, forms cognizable by the eye . . . sounds cognizable by the ear . . . odors cognizable by the nose . . . tastes cognizable by the tongue . . . tactile objects cognizable by the body . . . mental objects cognizable by the mind that are wished for, desired, agreeable, of a pleasing nature, connected with sensuality, enticing.

"If a monk delights in them, welcomes them, and remains holding to them, he is called 'a monk who has swallowed Māra's bait,' who has incurred misery, has incurred disaster, who is to be done with by the Evil One as he desires.

"There are, monks, forms cognizable by the eye . . . mental objects cognizable by the mind that are wished for, desired, agreeable, of a pleasing nature, connected with sensuality, enticing. If a monk does not delight in them, does not welcome them, and does not remain holding to them, he is called 'a monk who has not swallowed Māra's bait, who broke the hook, who destroyed the hook,' who has not incurred misery, not incurred disaster, who is not to be done with by the Evil One as he desires."

12. *Koṭṭhikasutta*
Koṭṭhika (SN 35:232 [191]; IV 162–65)

On one occasion the Venerable Sāriputta and the Venerable Mahākoṭṭhika were dwelling at Bārāṇasī in Isipatana, in the deer park. Then, in the evening, the Venerable Mahākoṭṭhita emerged from seclusion, approached the Venerable Sāriputta, and exchanged greetings with him. When they had concluded their greetings and cordial talk, he sat down to one side and said this to the Venerable Sāriputta: "How is it, friend Sāriputta, is the eye the fetter of forms or are forms the fetter of the eye? Is the ear the fetter of sounds or are sounds the fetter of the ear? Is the nose the fetter of odors or are odors the fetter of the nose? Is the tongue the fetter of tastes or are tastes the fetter of the tongue? Is the body the fetter of tactile objects or are tactile objects the fetter of the body? Is the mind the fetter of mental objects or are mental objects the fetter of the mind?"

"Friend Koṭṭhita, the eye is not the fetter of forms nor are forms the fetter of the eye, but the desire-and-lust that arises there in dependence on both of these: that is the fetter there. . . . The mind is not the fetter of mental objects nor are mental objects the fetter of the mind, but the desire-and-lust that arises there in dependence on both of these: that is the fetter there.

"Suppose, friend, a black ox and a white ox were yoked together by a single harness or yoke. If one were to say, 'The black ox is the fetter of the white ox; the white ox is the fetter of the black ox,' would one speaking thus speak rightly?"

"No indeed, friend. The black ox, friend, is not the fetter of the white ox, nor is the white ox the fetter of the black ox, but rather the single harness or yoke by which the two are yoked together: that is the fetter there."

"So too, friend, the eye is not the fetter of forms nor are forms the fetter of the eye, but the desire-and-lust that arises there in dependence on both of these: that is the fetter there. . . . The mind is not the fetter of mental objects nor are mental objects the fetter of the mind, but the desire-and-lust that arises there in dependence on both of these: that is the fetter there.

"If, friend, the eye were the fetter of forms or if forms were the fetter of the eye, this living of the spiritual life would not be discerned for the complete destruction of suffering. But since the eye is not the fetter of forms nor are forms the fetter of the eye—but the desire-and-lust that arises there in dependence on both is the fetter there—the living of the spiritual life is discerned for the complete destruction of suffering. . . .

"If the mind were the fetter of mental objects or if mental objects were the fetter of the mind, this living of the spiritual life would not be discerned for the complete destruction of suffering. But since the mind is not the fetter of mental objects nor are mental objects the fetter of the mind—but the desire-and-lust that arises there in dependence on both is the fetter there—the living of the spiritual life is discerned for the complete destruction of suffering.

"In this way too, friend, it can be understood how the eye is not the fetter of forms nor forms the fetter of the eye, but the desire-and-lust that arises there in dependence on both: that is the fetter there . . . how the mind is not the fetter of mental objects nor mental objects the fetter of the mind, but the desire-and-lust that arises there in dependence on both: that is the fetter there.

"There exists, friend, in the Blessed One the eye, the Blessed One sees a form with the eye, but for the Blessed One there is no desire-and-lust; the Blessed One is well liberated in mind. There exists in the Blessed One the ear, the Blessed One hears a sound with the ear, but for the Blessed One there is no desire-and-lust; the Blessed One is well liberated in mind. There exists in the Blessed One the nose, the Blessed One smells an odor with the nose, but for the Blessed One there is no desire-and-lust; the Blessed One is well liberated in mind. There exists in the Blessed One the tongue, the Blessed One experiences a taste with the tongue, but for the Blessed One there is no desire-and-lust; the Blessed One is well liberated in mind. There exists in the Blessed One the body, the Blessed One feels a tactile object with the body, but for the Blessed One there is no desire-and-lust; the Blessed One is well liberated in mind. There exists in the Blessed One the mind, the Blessed One cognizes a mental object with the mind, but for the Blessed One there is no desire-and-lust; the Blessed One is well liberated in mind.

"In this way, friend, it can be understood how the eye is not the fetter of forms nor forms the fetter of the eye, but the desire-and-lust that arises there in dependence on both: that is the fetter there . . . how the mind is not the fetter of mental objects nor mental objects the fetter of the mind, but the desire-and-lust that arises there in dependence on both: that is the fetter there."

13. *Dārukkhandhopamasutta*
Simile of the Log (SN 35:241 [200]; IV 179–81)

On one occasion the Blessed One was dwelling at Kosambī on the bank of the Ganges River. The Blessed One saw a great log being swept along by the stream of the Ganges River and addressed the monks: "Do you see, monks, that great log being swept along by the stream of the Ganges River?"—"Yes, Bhante."

"If, monks, that log does not approach the near bank, does not approach the far bank, does not sink in the middle; if it is not cast up on high ground; if humans do not grab it, if non-humans do not grab it, if whirlpools do not grab it, if it does not become inwardly rotten, in such a case that log will slant toward the ocean, slope toward the ocean, incline toward the ocean. For what reason? Because the stream of the Ganges River slants toward the ocean, slopes toward the ocean, inclines toward the ocean.

"Just so, monks, if you too do not approach the near bank, do not approach the far bank, do not sink in the middle; if you are not cast up on high ground; if humans do not grab you, if non-humans do not grab you, if whirlpools do not grab you, if you do not become inwardly rotten, in such a case you will slant toward nibbāna, slope toward nibbāna, incline toward nibbāna. For what reason? Because, monks, right view slants toward nibbāna, slopes toward nibbāna, inclines toward nibbāna."

When such was said, a certain monk said to the Blessed One: "What, Bhante, is the near bank, what is the far bank, what is sinking in the middle, what is being cast up on high ground, what is the human grasp, what is the non-human grasp, what is the grasp of a whirlpool, what is inward rottenness?"

"'The near bank,' monk: this is a designation for the six internal sense bases. 'The far bank': this is a designation for the six external sense bases. 'Sinking in the middle': this is a designation for delight and lust. 'Being cast up on high ground': this is a designation for the conceit 'I am.'

"And what, monk, is the human grasp? Here, a monk bonds with laypeople, delighting together, sorrowing together, happy when they are happy, miserable when they are miserable; when duties and tasks have arisen [for those laypeople], he exerts himself in them. This is called the 'human grasp.'

"And what, monk, is the non-human grasp? Here, someone lives the spiritual life with a wish for [rebirth into] a certain company of devas: 'By this good behavior or observance or austerity or spiritual life I will become a deva or a certain one among the devas.' This is called the 'non-human grasp.' 'The whirlpool grasp': this is a designation for the five objects of sensual pleasure.

"And what, monk, is inward rottenness? Here, someone is of bad behavior, of an evil nature, of impure suspect behavior, concealing his action, not an ascetic but claiming to be an ascetic, not celibate but claiming to be celibate, inwardly rotten, corrupt, rubbish. This is called 'inward rottenness.'"

Now on that occasion the cowherd Nanda was standing not far from the Blessed One. He said this to the Blessed One: "Bhante, I do not approach the near bank, I do not approach the far bank, I will not sink in the middle. I will not be cast up on high ground; humans will not grab me, non-humans will not grab me, a whirlpool will not grab me. I will not become inwardly rotten. Bhante, I would obtain the going forth in the presence of the Blessed One; I would obtain ordination."

"In that case, Nanda, return the cows to the owners."

"The cows will go, Bhante, longing for their calves."

"Return the cows to the owners, Nanda."

Then the cowherd Nanda returned the cows to the owners, approached the Blessed One, and said this: "Bhante, the cows have been returned to the owners. I would obtain the going forth in the presence of the Blessed One; I would obtain ordination."

The cowherd Nanda obtained the going forth in the presence of the Blessed One; he obtained ordination. And not long after he was ordained, dwelling alone, withdrawn, heedful, ardent, and resolute, the Venerable Nanda, in no long time, by realizing it for himself with direct knowledge, in this present life entered and dwelled in that unsurpassed goal of the spiritual life for the sake of which young people rightly go forth from the household life into homelessness. He directly knew: "Finished is birth, the spiritual life has been lived, what had to be done has been done, there is no further for this state of being." And the Venerable Nanda became one of the arahants.

14. *Vīṇopamasutta*
Simile of the Lute (SN 35:246 [205]; IV 195–98)

"If, monks, in any monk or nun desire or lust or hatred or delusion or aversion of mind should arise in regard to forms cognizable by the eye, they should rein in the mind from them thus: 'This path is fearful, dangerous, strewn with thorns, covered by jungle, a deviant path, an evil path, a way beset by scarcity. This is a path followed by inferior people; it is not the path followed by superior people. This is not for you.' In this way the mind should be reined in from these states regarding forms cognizable by the eye. So too regarding sounds cognizable by the ear . . . regarding mental objects cognizable by the mind.

"Suppose, monks, that the barley has ripened and the watchman is negligent. If a bull enters the barley field, he might indulge himself as much as he likes. So too, the uninstructed worldling who does not exercise restraint over the six bases for contact indulges as much as he likes in the five cords of sensual pleasure. But suppose that the barley has ripened and the watchman is vigilant. If a bull enters the barley field, the watchman would catch hold of him firmly by the muzzle, get a secure grip on the locks between his horns, and, keeping him in check, would give him a sound beating with his staff. Then he would drive the bull away. This might happen a second time and a third time. But eventually that bull, remembering the beating, would not enter that barley field again. So too, when a monk's mind has been subdued, well subdued, regarding the six bases for contact, it then becomes inwardly steady, settled, unified, and concentrated.

"Suppose, monks, a king or a king's chief minister had never before heard the sound of a lute. He would hear the sound of a lute and would say thus: 'Hey, of what is this the sound, which is so enticing, so lovely, so intoxicating, so infatuating, so captivating?'

"They would tell him: 'This, sire, is what is called a lute, whose sound is so enticing, so lovely, so intoxicating, so infatuating, so captivating.' He would say thus: 'Go, men, bring that lute to me.' They would bring that lute to him.

"They would tell him: 'This, sire, is that lute whose sound is so enticing, so lovely, so intoxicating, so infatuating, so captivating.' He would say: 'Enough for me with that lute, men. Bring me that sound itself.'

"They would tell him: 'This lute, sire, is made up of numerous components, of a great many components. When played upon with its numerous components, it makes music—that is, in dependence on the belly, the parchment, the arm, the support, the strings, the plectrum, and a person's appropriate effort. Thus, sire, this lute is made up of numerous components, of a great many components. When played upon with its numerous components, it makes music.'

"He would split the lute into ten pieces or a hundred pieces. Having split it into ten pieces or a hundred pieces, he would reduce these to splinters. Having reduced these to splinters, he would burn them in a fire and reduce them to ashes. Having reduced them to ashes, he would winnow the ashes in a strong wind or have them carried off by a river with a swift current. Then he would say: 'Non-existing indeed, men, is this thing called a lute, as well as anything else called a lute. The multitude are extremely heedless and confused about this!'

"So too, monks, a monk investigates form as far as there is the range of form; he investigates feeling as far as there is the range of feeling; he investigates perception as far as there is the range of perception; he investigates volitional activities as far as there is the range of volitional activities; he investigates consciousness as far as there is the range of consciousness. As he is investigating, those [notions of] 'I' or 'mine' or 'I am' that occurred to him before no longer occur to him."

15. *Chappāṇakopamasutta*
Simile of the Six Animals (SN 35:247 [206]; IV 198–200)

[1. Non-restraint]
"Suppose, monks, a man with wounded and festering limbs would enter a woods of sharp reeds. The kusa thorns would pierce his feet and the reed blades would scratch his limbs. Thus on that account the man would experience pain and dejection to an even greater extent.

"Just so, monks, some monk here, gone to the village or the forest, would meet someone who reproaches him thus: 'This monk, acting in such a way, behaving in such a way, is an impure village thorn.' Having known him thus as 'a thorn,' one should understand the meaning of restraint and non-restraint.

"And how, monks, does non-restraint occur? Here, having seen a form with the eye, a monk is intent upon a pleasant form and annoyed by an unpleasant form. He dwells without having established mindfulness of the body, with a limited mind, and he does not understand as it really is that liberation of mind, liberation by wisdom, where those arisen bad unwholesome qualities of his cease without remainder.

"Having cognized a sound with the ear . . . an odor with the nose . . . a taste with the tongue . . . a tactile object with the body . . . a mental object with the mind, a monk is intent upon a pleasant mental object and annoyed by an unpleasant mental object. He dwells without having established mindfulness of the body, with a limited mind, and he does not understand as it really is that liberation of mind, liberation by wisdom, where those arisen bad unwholesome qualities of his cease without remainder.

"Suppose, monks, a man would catch six animals that had different domains and different feeding grounds, and he would bind them with a strong rope. Having caught a snake, he would bind it with a strong rope. Having caught a crocodile, he would bind it with a strong rope. Having caught a bird, he would bind it with a strong rope. Having caught a dog, he would bind it with a strong rope. Having caught a jackal, he would bind it with a strong rope. Having caught a monkey, he would bind it with a strong rope. Having bound them with a strong rope, he would make a knot in the middle and let go.

"Then those six animals that had different domains and different feeding grounds would each pull toward their own feeding ground and domain. The snake would pull, thinking: 'I will enter an anthill'; the crocodile would pull, thinking: 'I will enter the water'; the bird would pull, thinking: 'I will fly to the sky'; the dog would pull, thinking: 'I will enter a village'; the jackal would pull, thinking: 'I will enter a charnel ground'; the monkey would pull, thinking: 'I will enter the woods.'

"When those six animals have become weakened and fatigued, they would follow the strongest animal among them; they would submit to it and come under its control.

"Just so, monks, when for any monk mindfulness directed to the body is undeveloped and uncultivated, the eye pulls him toward agreeable forms and disagreeable forms are repulsive; the ear pulls him toward agreeable sounds and disagreeable sounds are repulsive; the nose pulls him toward agreeable odors and disagreeable odors are repulsive; the tongue pulls him toward agreeable tastes and disagreeable tastes are repulsive; the body pulls him toward agreeable tactile objects and disagreeable tactile objects are repulsive; the mind pulls him toward agreeable mental objects and disagreeable mental objects are repulsive. Thus non-restraint occurs.

[2. Restraint]

"And how, monks, does restraint occur? Here, monks, having seen a form with the eye, a monk is not intent upon a pleasant form and is not annoyed by an unpleasant form. He dwells with mindfulness of the body established, with a measureless mind, and he understands as it really is that liberation of mind, liberation by wisdom, where those arisen bad unwholesome qualities of his cease without remainder.

"Having cognized a sound with the ear . . . an odor with the nose . . . a taste with the tongue . . . a tactile object with the body . . . a mental object with the mind, a monk is not intent upon a pleasant mental object and is not annoyed by an unpleasant mental object. He dwells with mindfulness of the body established, with a measureless mind, and he understands as it really is that liberation of mind, liberation by wisdom, where those arisen bad unwholesome qualities of his cease without remainder.

"Suppose, monks, a man would catch six animals that had different domains and different feeding grounds, and he would bind them with a strong rope. Having caught a snake, he would bind it with a strong rope. . . . Having caught a monkey, he would bind it with a strong rope. Having bound them with a strong rope, he would tie it to a strong post or pillar. Then those six animals that had different domains and different feeding grounds would each pull toward their own feeding ground and domain. The snake would pull, [thinking]: 'I will enter an anthill' . . . the monkey would pull, [thinking]: 'I will enter the woods.'

"When those six animals have become weakened and fatigued, they would stand near that same post or pillar, sit near it, lie down near it.

"Just so, monks, when for any monk mindfulness directed to the body is developed and cultivated, the eye does not pull him toward agreeable forms and disagreeable forms are not repulsive; the ear does not pull him toward agreeable sounds and disagreeable sounds are not repulsive; the nose does not pull him toward agreeable odors and disagreeable odors are not repulsive; the tongue does not pull him toward agreeable tastes and disagreeable tastes are not repulsive; the body does not pull him toward agreeable tactile objects and disagreeable tactile objects are not repulsive; the mind does not pull him toward agreeable mental objects and disagreeable mental objects are not repulsive. Thus restraint occurs.

"'A strong post or pillar,' monks: this is a designation for mindfulness directed to the body. Therefore, monks, you should train thus: 'Mindfulness directed to the body will be developed and cultivated by us, made a vehicle, made a basis, stabilized, repeated, and well undertaken.' Thus indeed, monks, you should train."

4. Dependent Origination: The Origination and Cessation of Suffering

Introduction

The teaching of dependent origination offers a more detailed perspective on the causal dynamics maintaining saṃsāra, the round of rebirths. The Pāli term *paṭiccasamuppāda* is a compound of *paṭicca*, the absolutive of *pacceti*, "comes back to, falls back on, relies on," and the noun *samuppāda*, "origination." The common translation of *paṭiccasamuppāda* as "interdependent co-arising" (and its variants) is, strictly speaking, inaccurate. While certain pairs of factors in the formula may be mutually dependent, the word *paṭicca* itself does not imply mutuality but the dependence of one factor upon the other. Again, *samuppāda* does not mean simultaneous arising. While certain factors may arise simultaneously (for instance, contact and feeling), others, such as feeling and craving, may be separated by a temporal gap, and others, such as birth and old-age-and-death,[44] are necessarily separated by a temporal gap.

The formula for dependent origination is founded upon an abstract "structural principle" stipulating the general law that things arise through conditions. As stated in **4.6**, **4.7**, and **4.10**, the principle runs thus: "When this exists, that comes to be; with the arising of this, that arises. When this does not exist, that does not come to be; with the cessation of this, that ceases."[45] In the suttas, this principle is applied in a variety of ways, but the main application is to a sequence of twelve factors, each of which arises in dependence on its predecessor and ceases with the ceasing of its predecessor. The teaching can thus be seen as an expanded version of the second and third noble truths, showing in finer detail the chain of conditions responsible for the origination and cessation of dukkha.[46]

The diagnosis of dukkha offered by this formula probes more deeply into the issue of origins than the standard statement of the second noble truth, for it reveals, lying at the very base of repeated existence, a more fundamental condition than craving. This more fundamental condition is *avijjā*, ignorance. Though defined narrowly in the suttas as "not knowing suffering, its origin, its cessation, and the path," ignorance represents more broadly the lack of awareness of all the principles that illuminate the true nature of phenomena. These include not only the four truths but the three characteristics and dependent origination itself. Ignorance sustains the round of dukkha, and when ignorance comes to an end, the entire network of conditions also ends, culminating in "the cessation of this whole mass of suffering."

The individual factors that constitute the formula of dependent origination are formally defined in **4.1**, but the suttas leave us only with these definitions, without demonstrating precisely how the factors hang together as an integral whole. This ambiguity has led to the emergence of different, sometimes competing interpretations of the formula. However, virtually all the ancient Indian Buddhist schools concur that the formula shows the sequence of causal factors that sustain the round of rebirths as extended over a series of lives. Some modern interpreters have challenged this interpretation, holding that the entire sequence of twelve factors pertains to a single life. The Vibhaṅga (of the Abhidhamma Piṭaka) does have a section showing how dependent origination operates at the level of individual mind-moments, but to suit its purpose this version alters the definitions of some of the factors, especially "existence," "birth," "old age," and "death."[47] Apart from this special application, it seems clear enough that, as originally intended, the twelve terms of the formula are spread out over multiple lives.

The traditional explanation, stated simply and concisely, goes like this: Because of fundamental *ignorance*, one engages in various *volitional activities*—wholesome and unwholesome bodily, verbal, or purely mental actions—that generate kamma with the potential to produce a new existence. These karmic activities, at death, propel *consciousness* into a new existence. The new existence begins when consciousness arrives at a new embodiment, bringing forth a fresh assemblage of bodily and mental phenomena, which are collectively designated *name-and-form*.[48] As name-and-form matures, the *six sense bases* take shape and begin to function. When the sense bases encounter their corresponding objects, *contact* occurs. Contact gives rise to *feeling* through the six bases—pleasant, painful, and neutral feelings, which trigger corresponding responses. In an untrained person, feeling arouses *craving*, a desire to obtain pleasant objects and avoid situations that cause pain. When one obtains the objects of desire, one relishes them and holds to them tightly; this is *clinging*, an intensification of craving, which may also find expression in views that justify one's craving for more pleasure and continued existence. Through clinging, one engages in a fresh round of volitional activities that create the potential for a new *existence*—an existence that may occur in any of the three realms recognized by Buddhist cosmology: the desire realm, the realm of subtle form, and the formless realm. That new existence begins with *birth*, and once birth takes place, there follows *old-age-and-death* and all the other manifestations of dukkha encountered in the course of existence.

The three-life interpretation of dependent origination has sometimes been branded a commentarial invention on the ground that the suttas themselves do not divide the terms up into different lifetimes. However, while it is true that we do not find in the suttas an explicit distribution of the factors into three lives, close examination of the variants on the standard formula lends strong support to the three-life interpretation.[49] One example is SN 12:19 (at II 23–25), where it is said that both the fool and the sage have acquired a body through the ignorance and craving of the past. The fool does not eliminate ignorance and craving and so, following the breakup of the present body, the fool moves on to a new embodied existence, once again subject to birth, old age, and death. The sage eliminates present ignorance and craving and is thus freed from any future embodied existence, no longer bound to birth, old age, and death. This statement clearly assigns certain factors to the past, their results to the present, and the results of present activity to the future.

The twelve-factored formula was never intended to be exclusively linear but to serve as a simplified representation of a complex process that involves overlapping and intersecting lines of conditionality. The extraction of twelve conditions and their configuration in the familiar sequence might be considered an expository device intended to show the causal dynamics underlying the round of rebirths. To convey a clearer understanding of the relationships among the twelve factors, the commentarial tradition explains that the factors can be assigned to four groups, each with five factors.[50]

(1) When ignorance and volitional activities were present in the past life, craving, clinging, and the karmically active phase of existence were also present. These five constitute *the causal group of the past existence.*

(2) These five "propulsive" causes functioned in unison to bring forth consciousness and name-and-form, which arise at the initial moment of the present existence and continue to evolve in uninterrupted interplay through the entire course of life. From their interplay, the six sense bases, contact, and feeling emerge. These five constitute *the resultant group of the present existence.*

(3) These five in turn serve as the grounds for a new round of craving, clinging, and karmic activities tending toward a new existence. When these arise, ignorance necessarily underlies them, and what is referred to as karmic existence is essentially identical with volitional activities. These are the *five causal factors of the present existence.*

(4) These five as causes bring forth a new fivefold set of resultant factors in the future—namely, consciousness, name-and-form, the six sense bases, contact, and feeling. These make up *the resultant group of the future existence.*

The five factors making up each resultant group necessarily undergo the stages of physiological development and decline, and thus birth along with old-age-and-death—the last two factors in the twelvefold series—are implicitly contained within the resultant groups.

Looked at from another angle, ignorance and craving jointly function as the roots of the entire process of saṃsāra. Along with clinging, these three constitute *the round of defilements*. Two factors, volitional activities and the karmically active phase of existence, constitute *the round of kamma*. And the resultant phase of existence, along with all the remaining factors, constitute *the round of results*.[51]

3 periods	*12 factors*	*20 modes in 4 groups*
Past	1. Ignorance 2. Volitional activities	Past causes 5: 1, 2, 8, 9, 10
Present	3. Consciousness 4. Name-and-form 5. Six sense bases 6. Contact 7. Feeling	Present effects 5: 3–7
	8. Craving 9. Clinging 10. Existence	Present causes 5: 8, 9, 10, 1, 2
Future	11. Birth 12. Old-age-and-death	Future effects 5: 3–7

The suttas do not offer such a detailed account of dependent origination, but provide instead different perspectives on this teaching. The chain of conditions is said at **4.5** to be a natural law that remains valid whether or not buddhas arise in the world. This sequence of conditions—called "specific conditionality" (*idappaccayatā*)—persists as a fixed principle, stable and invariable through all time, said to be "real, not unreal, not otherwise." The task of a buddha is to penetrate this law and fully comprehend it, and then to elucidate it for others.

Several suttas in this collection show the realization of dependent origination to have been the great discovery the Buddha made on the night of his enlightenment. One text included here, **4.2**, states this with respect to the present buddha, Gotama. The preceding suttas in that series relate the same narrative about his six predecessors. He begins his investigation seeking an outlet from the suffering inherent in old age and death. His inquiry takes him back through the sequence until he arrives at the most fundamental condition behind the whole series—namely, ignorance. The discernment of each link binding conditions together is here said to have come about through the application of "thorough attention," culminating in "a breakthrough by wisdom." The discernment of the entire chain, in the orders of both origination and cessation, marked the gaining of the eye of knowledge. In **4.11**, we find a different take on the same line of inquiry, with the series ending in the mutual conditioning of consciousness and name-and-form. In this version the Buddha declares that after seeing how consciousness and name-and-form are mutually dependent and how each ceases with the ceasing of the other, he had discovered the path to enlightenment.

Dependent origination offers a dynamic perspective on nonself that complements the analytic approach provided by the critical examination of the five aggregates. The formula shows how the process of rebirth and the working of karmic causation occur without an underlying subject, a substantial self, passing through the successive stages of life and migrating from one existence to the next. In the Buddha's time, philosophers and contemplatives were divided into two opposed camps. One camp, the eternalists, held that at the core of every person there is an immortal self—substantial and autonomous—that persists through the cycle of rebirths and attains liberation, preserving its unchanging essence. The other camp, the annihilationists, denied the existence of a permanent self that survives bodily death. They held that with the breakup of the body, personal existence comes to an absolute end and thus at death the living being is utterly annihilated. Dependent origination, as **4.4** demonstrates, served the Buddha as a "teaching by the middle" that avoids these two extremes. It avoids the extreme that "all exists," a statement of eternalism, by showing how personal continuity is possible without a self that persists through the process. And it avoids the extreme that "all does not exist," the claim of the annihilationists, by showing that so long as the conditions that drive the process of becoming remain intact, the conditions will continue to operate, stitching together one life to the next.

The suttas selected here are noteworthy not only for the various angles they present on dependent origination but also for their rich variety of similes. Thus **4.8** uses the simile of the clay pot to illustrate the arahant's attainment of final nibbāna. The simile in **4.9** illustrates the two sides of dependent origination with the sustenance and destruction of the tree. In **4.10** the Buddha compares the ever-fickle mind to a monkey that roams through a forest by grabbing and releasing one branch after another. In **4.11** he compares his discovery of the noble eightfold path to a man wandering through a forest who comes across an ancient path leading to an ancient city, which he has the king restore to its previous glory. And in **4.12** he uses the simile of the cup of poisoned beverage to demonstrate how those ascetics who nurture craving remain bound to the round of birth and death, while those who abandon craving win liberation from suffering, like the person who rejects the poisoned beverage and thereby preserves his life.

1. *Vibhaṅgasutta*
Analysis (SN 12:2; II 2–4)

"I will teach you, monks, dependent origination and I will analyze it for you. Listen and attend well. I will speak."—"Yes, Bhante," those monks replied. The Blessed One said this:

"And what, monks, is dependent origination? With ignorance as condition, monks, volitional activities [come to be]; with volitional activities as condition, consciousness; with consciousness as condition, name-and-form; with name-and-form as condition, the six sense bases; with the six sense bases as condition, contact; with contact as condition, feeling; with feeling as condition, craving; with craving as condition, clinging; with clinging as condition, existence; with existence as condition, birth; with birth as condition, old-age-and-death, sorrow, lamentation, pain, dejection, and misery come to be. Such is the origin of this whole mass of suffering.

"And what, monks, is old-age-and-death? The aging of the various beings in the various orders of beings, their growing old, brokenness of teeth, grayness of hair, wrinkling of skin, decline of vitality, degeneration of the faculties: this is called old age. The passing away of the various beings from the various orders of beings, their perishing, breakup, disappearance, mortality, death, completion of time, the breakup of the aggregates, the laying down of the carcass: this is called death. Thus this old age and this death are together called old-age-and-death.

"And what, monks, is birth? The birth of the various beings into the various orders of beings, their being born, descent, production, the manifestation of the aggregates, the obtaining of the sense bases. This is called birth.

"And what, monks, is existence? There are these three kinds of existence: desire-realm existence, form-realm existence, formless-realm existence.[52] This is called existence.

"And what, monks, is clinging? There are these four kinds of clinging: clinging to sensual pleasures, clinging to views, clinging to precepts and observances, clinging to a doctrine of self. This is called clinging.

"And what, monks, is craving? There are these six classes of craving: craving for forms, craving for sounds, craving for odors, craving for tastes, craving for tactile objects, craving for mental objects. This is called craving.

"And what, monks, is feeling? There are these six classes of feeling: feeling born of eye-contact, feeling born of ear-contact, feeling born of nose-contact, feeling born of tongue-contact, feeling born of body-contact, feeling born of mind-contact. This is called feeling.

"And what, monks, is contact? There are these six classes of contact: eye-contact, ear-contact, nose-contact, tongue-contact, body-contact, mind-contact. This is called contact.

"And what, monks, are the six sense bases? The eye-base, the ear-base, the nose-base, the tongue-base, the body-base, the mind-base. These are called the six sense bases.

"And what, monks, is name-and-form? Feeling, perception, volition, contact, attention: this is called name.[53] The four great elements and the form derived from the four great elements: this is called form. Thus this name and this form are together called name-and-form.

"And what, monks, is consciousness? There are these six classes of consciousness: eye-consciousness, ear-consciousness, nose-consciousness, tongue-consciousness, body-consciousness, mind-consciousness. This is called consciousness.

"And what, monks, are volitional activities? There are these three kinds of volitional activities: bodily volitional activity, verbal volitional activity, mental volitional activity.[54] These are called volitional activities.

"And what, monks, is ignorance? Not knowing suffering, not knowing the origin of suffering, not knowing the cessation of suffering, not knowing the way leading to the cessation of suffering. This is called ignorance.

"Thus, monks, with ignorance as condition, volitional activities come to be; with volitional activities as condition, consciousness.... Such is the origin of this whole mass of suffering.

"But with the remainderless fading away and cessation of ignorance there is cessation of volitional activities; with the cessation of volitional activities, cessation of consciousness; with the cessation of consciousness, cessation of name-and-form; with the cessation of name-and-form, cessation of the six sense bases; with the cessation of the six sense bases, cessation of contact; with the cessation of contact, cessation of feeling; with the cessation of feeling, cessation of craving, with the cessation of craving, cessation of clinging; with the cessation of clinging, cessation of existence; with the cessation of existence, cessation of birth; with the cessation of birth, old-age-and-death, sorrow, lamentation, pain, dejection, and misery cease. Such is the cessation of this whole mass of suffering."

This is what the Blessed One said. Elated, those monks delighted in the Blessed One's statement.

2. *Gotamasutta*
Gotama (SN 12:10; II 10–11)

[1. Origination]
"Before the enlightenment, monks, while I was just a bodhisatta, not fully enlightened, this occurred to me: 'Alas, this world has fallen into trouble; it is born, grows old, and dies, it passes away and is reborn, yet it does not understand the escape from this suffering, from old-age-and-death. When now will an escape be discerned from this suffering, from old-age-and-death?'

"Then, monks, this occurred to me: 'When what exists does old-age-and-death come to be? By what is old-age-and-death conditioned?' Then, through thorough attention,[55] there took place in me a breakthrough by wisdom: 'When there is birth, old-age-and-death comes to be; with birth as condition, there is old-age-and-death.'

"Then, monks, this occurred to me: 'When what exists does birth come to be . . . existence . . . clinging . . . craving . . . feeling . . . contact . . . the six sense bases . . . name-and-form . . . consciousness . . . do volitional activities come to be? By what are volitional activities conditioned?' Then, through thorough attention, there took place in me a breakthrough by wisdom: 'When there is ignorance, volitional activities come to be; with ignorance as condition, there are volitional activities.'

"Thus this indeed is so: With ignorance as condition, volitional activities come to be; with volitional activities as condition, consciousness. . . . Such is the origin of this whole mass of suffering.

"'Origin, origin'—thus, monks, in regard to things unheard before, the eye arose in me, knowledge arose, wisdom arose, clear knowledge arose, light arose.

[2. Cessation]

"Then, monks, this occurred to me: 'When what does not exist does old-age-and-death not come to be? With the cessation of what is there cessation of old-age-and-death?' Then, through thorough attention, there took place in me a breakthrough by wisdom: 'When there is no birth, old-age-and-death does not come to be; with the cessation of birth there is cessation of old-age-and-death.'

"Then, monks, this occurred to me: 'When what does not exist does birth not come to be . . . existence . . . clinging . . . craving . . . feeling . . . contact . . . the six sense bases . . . name-and-form . . . consciousness . . . volitional activities not come to be? With the cessation of what is there cessation of volitional activities?' Then, through thorough attention, there took place in me a breakthrough by wisdom: 'When there is no ignorance, volitional activities do not come to be; with the cessation of ignorance there is cessation of volitional activities.'

"Thus this indeed is so: With the cessation of ignorance there is cessation of volitional activities; with the cessation of volitional activities, cessation of consciousness. . . . Such is the cessation of this whole mass of suffering.

"'Cessation, cessation'—thus, monks, in regard to things unheard before, the eye arose in me, knowledge arose, wisdom arose, clear knowledge arose, light arose."

3. *Moḷiyaphaggunasutta*
Moḷiyaphagguna (SN 12:12, II 12–14)

[1. The four kinds of nutriment]
"There are, monks, these four nutriments for the persistence of beings that have come to be or for the assistance of those approaching [a new] existence. What four? Edible nutriment coarse or subtle, contact second, mental volition third, and consciousness fourth.[56] These are the four nutriments for the persistence of beings that have come to be or for the assistance of those approaching [a new] existence."

[2. Who consumes consciousness?]
When such was said, the Venerable Moḷiyaphagguna said this to the Blessed One: "Who, Bhante, consumes the consciousness nutriment?"[57]

"Not a proper question," the Blessed One said: "I do not say: '[Someone] consumes.' If I would say, '[Someone] consumes,' in that case it would be a proper question: 'Who, Bhante, consumes?' But I do not say thus. Since I do not say thus, one should ask me: 'For what, Bhante, is the consciousness-nutriment [a condition]?' This is a proper question. The proper answer there is: 'The consciousness-nutriment is a condition for the production of renewed existence in the future. When there is that which has come-to-be, there are the six sense bases; with the six sense bases as condition, there is contact.'"

[3. From contact to clinging]
"Who, Bhante, contacts?"—"Not a proper question," the Blessed One said. "I do not say: '[Someone] contacts.' If I would say, '[Someone] contacts,' there would be a proper question: 'Who, Bhante, contacts?' But I do not say thus. Since I do not say thus, one should ask me: 'Through what condition, Bhante, is there contact?' This is a proper question. The proper answer there is: 'With the six sense bases as condition there is contact; with contact as condition there is feeling.'"

"Who, Bhante, feels?"—"Not a proper question," the Blessed One said. "I do not say: '[Someone] feels.' If I would say, '[Someone] feels,' there would be a proper question: 'Who, Bhante, feels?' But I do not say thus. Since I do not say thus, one should ask me: 'Through what condition, Bhante, is there feeling?' This is a proper question. The proper answer there is: 'With contact as condition there is feeling; with feeling as condition there is craving.'"

"Who, Bhante, craves?"—"Not a proper question," the Blessed One said. "I do not say: '[Someone] craves.' If I would say, '[Someone] craves,' there would be a proper question: 'Who, Bhante, craves?' But I do not say thus. Since I do not say thus, one should ask me: 'Through what condition, Bhante, is there craving?' This is a proper question. The proper answer there is: 'With feeling as condition there is craving; with craving as condition there is clinging.'"

"Who, Bhante, clings?"—"Not a proper question," the Blessed One said. "I do not say: '[Someone] clings.' If I would say, '[Someone] clings,' there would be a proper question: 'Who, Bhante, clings?' But I do not say thus. Since I do not say thus, one should ask me: 'Through what condition, Bhante, is there clinging?' This is a proper question. The proper answer there is: 'With craving as condition there is clinging; with clinging as condition there is existence. . . .' Such is the origin of this whole mass of suffering.

[4. Cessation]

"But, Phagguna, with the remainderless fading away and cessation of the six bases of contact, there is cessation of contact; with the cessation of contact, cessation of feeling; with the cessation of feeling, cessation of craving; with the cessation of craving, cessation of clinging; with the cessation of clinging, cessation of existence; with the cessation of existence, cessation of birth; with the cessation of birth, old-age-and-death, sorrow, lamentation, pain, dejection, and misery cease. Such is the cessation of this whole mass of suffering."

4. *Kaccānagottasutta*
Kaccānagotta (SN 12:15; II 16–17)

Then the Venerable Kaccānagotta approached the Blessed One, paid homage to him, sat down to one side, and said this: "Bhante, it is said, 'right view, right view.' In what way, Bhante, does right view occur?"

"This world, Kaccāna, for the most part is dependent upon a dyad—upon [the notions of] 'existence' and 'non-existence.'[58] But, Kaccāna, for one seeing the world's origin as it really is with correct wisdom, [the notion of] 'non-existence' does not occur in regard to the world. And for one seeing the world's cessation as it really is with correct wisdom, [the notion of] 'existence' does not occur in regard to the world.[59]

"This world, Kaccāna, is for the most part bound by involvement, clinging, and adherence. But this person does not approach, does not cling, does not stand upon that involvement, clinging, mental standpoint, adherence, and tendency, 'My self.' He is not perplexed and does not doubt that what arises is only suffering arising, that what ceases is suffering ceasing. Without dependence on others, knowledge about this occurs to him. It is in this way, Kaccāna, that right view occurs.

"'All exists': Kaccāna, this is one extreme. 'All does not exist': this is the second extreme. Not having approached both these extremes, the Tathāgata teaches the Dhamma by the middle: 'With ignorance as condition, volitional activities come to be; with volitional activities as condition, consciousness. . . . Such is the origin of this whole mass of suffering. But with the remainderless fading away and cessation of ignorance there is cessation of volitional activities; with the cessation of volitional activities, cessation of consciousness. . . . Such is the cessation of this whole mass of suffering.'"

5. *Paccayasutta*
Conditions (SN 12:20; II 25–26)

"I will teach you, monks, dependent origination and dependently originated phenomena. Listen to that and attend well. I will speak."—"Yes, Bhante," those monks replied. The Blessed One said this:

"And what, monks, is dependent origination? With birth as condition, old-age-and-death comes to be: whether there is an arising of tathāgatas or no arising of tathāgatas, that element still persists, the persistent pattern of phenomena, the lawfulness of phenomena, specific conditionality.[60] The Tathāgata becomes enlightened about this and breaks through to it. Having become enlightened about this, having broken through to it, he explains it, teaches it, points it out, establishes it, discloses it, analyzes it, elucidates it. And he says: 'See! With birth as condition, monks, old-age-and-death comes to be.'

"With existence as condition, birth comes to be. . . . With ignorance as condition, volitional activities come to be: whether there is an arising of tathāgatas or no arising of tathāgatas, that element still persists, the persistent pattern of phenomena, the lawfulness of phenomena, specific conditionality. The Tathāgata becomes enlightened about this and breaks through to it. Having become enlightened about this, having broken through to it, he explains it, teaches it, points it out, establishes it, discloses it, analyzes it, elucidates it. And he says: 'See! With ignorance as condition, monks, volitional activities come to be.'

"Thus, monks, the reality in that, the lack of unreality, the not-being otherwise, specific conditionality:[61] this is called dependent origination.

"And what, monks, are dependently originated phenomena? Old-age-and-death is impermanent, conditioned, dependently originated, subject to destruction, subject to vanishing, subject to fading away, subject to cessation. Birth. . . . Ignorance is impermanent, conditioned, dependently originated, subject to destruction, subject to vanishing, subject to fading away, subject to cessation. These are called dependently originated phenomena."

6. *Dasabalasutta*
Ten Powers (SN 12:22; II 28–29)

"The Tathāgata, monks, possessing the ten powers and possessing the four kinds of self-confidence,[62] claims the place of the chief bull, roars a lion's roar in the assemblies, and rolls the Brahma-wheel, saying: 'Such is form, such its origin, such its passing away; such is feeling, such its origin, such its passing away; such is perception, such its origin, such its passing away; such are volitional activities, such their origin, such their passing away; such is consciousness, such its origin, such its passing away.'

"Thus when this exists, that comes to be; with the arising of this, that arises. When this does not exist, that does not come to be; with the cessation of this, that ceases. That is, with ignorance as condition, volitional activities come to be; with volitional activities as condition, consciousness. . . . Such is the origin of this whole mass of suffering. But with the remainderless fading away and cessation of ignorance there is cessation of volitional activities; with the cessation of volitional activities, cessation of consciousness. . . . Such is the cessation of this whole mass of suffering.

"The Dhamma, monks, has thus been well expounded by me, elucidated, disclosed, revealed, stripped of patchwork. When the Dhamma has thus been well expounded by me, elucidated, disclosed, revealed, stripped of patchwork, this is surely enough for a young person who has gone forth out of faith to arouse energy thus: 'Willingly, let [only] my skin, sinews, and bones remain; let the flesh and blood in my body dry up, but so long as I have not attained whatever is to be attained by human strength, by human energy, by human exertion, there will be no stagnation of energy.'

"A lazy person, monks, dwells painfully, mixed with bad unwholesome qualities, and he discards great personal good. But an energetic person dwells happily, secluded from bad unwholesome qualities, and he fulfills great personal good. It is not by the inferior that there is the attainment of the foremost, but it is by the foremost that there is the attainment of the foremost. This spiritual life, monks, is a beverage of cream; the Teacher is present before you.

"Therefore, monks, arouse energy for the attainment of the as-yet-unattained, for the achievement of the as-yet-unachieved, for the realization of the as-yet-unrealized, [with the thought]: 'In such a way this going forth of ours will not be barren for us, but fruitful and valuable. As for those whose [gifts of] robes, alms food, lodgings, and medicinal requisites we use, these services they render us will be of great fruit and benefit [for them].' In such a way, monks, you should train.

"For by considering your own good, monks, it is enough to strive with heedfulness; by considering the good of others, it is enough to strive with heedfulness; by considering the good of both, it is enough to strive with heedfulness."

7. *Pañcaverabhayasutta*
Five Enemies and Perils (SN 12:41; II 68–69)

[1. A noble disciple's assurance]
Then the householder Anāthapiṇḍika approached the Blessed One, paid homage to him, and sat down to one side. The Blessed One then said this to the householder Anāthapiṇḍika:

"When, householder, for a noble disciple five perils and enemies have subsided, and he possesses the four factors of stream-entry, and the noble method has been well seen and well penetrated by him with wisdom, then, if he wishes he could by himself declare himself thus: 'I am one finished with hell, finished with the animal realm, finished with the domain of spirits, finished with the plane of misery, the bad destinations, the lower world. I am a stream-enterer, no longer subject to the lower world, fixed [in destiny], with enlightenment as my destination.'

[2. The five enemies and perils]
"What are the five perils and enemies that have subsided? Householder, one who destroys life, with the destruction of life as condition, engenders a peril and enemy pertaining to the present life and a peril and enemy pertaining to the future life, and he experiences mental pain and dejection. Thus for one who abstains from the destruction of life, this peril and enemy has subsided.

"One who takes what is not given. . . . One who engages in sexual misconduct. . . . One who speaks falsely. . . . One who indulges in liquor, wine, and intoxicants, a basis for heedlessness, with such indulgence as condition engenders a peril and enemy pertaining to the present life and a peril and enemy pertaining to the future life, and he experiences mental pain and dejection. Thus for one who abstains from indulgence in liquor, wine, and intoxicants, this peril and enemy has subsided. These are the five perils and enemies that have subsided.

[3. The four factors of stream-entry]
"What are the four factors of stream-entry that he possesses? Here, householder, the noble disciple possesses confirmed confidence in the Buddha thus: 'The Blessed One is an arah-

ant, perfectly enlightened, accomplished in clear knowledge and conduct, fortunate, knower of the world, unsurpassed trainer of persons to be tamed, teacher of devas and humans, the Enlightened One, the Blessed One.'

"He possesses confirmed confidence in the Dhamma thus: 'The Dhamma is well expounded by the Blessed One, directly visible, immediate, asking one to come and see, applicable, to be personally understood by the wise.'

"He possesses confirmed confidence in the Sangha thus: 'The Sangha of the Blessed One's disciples is practicing well, practicing in a straight way, practicing methodically, practicing properly—that is, the four pairs of persons, the eight types of individuals, this Sangha of the Blessed One's disciples is worthy of gifts, worthy of hospitality, worthy of offerings, worthy of salutation, the unsurpassed field of merit for the world.'

"He possesses the good behavior loved by the noble ones—unbroken, untorn, unblemished, unmottled, freeing, praised by the wise, ungrasped, leading to concentration. These are the four factors of stream-entry that he possesses.

[4. The noble method]

"And what is the noble method that he has well seen and well penetrated with wisdom? Here, householder, the noble disciple well attends thoroughly to dependent origination thus: 'When this exists, that comes to be; with the arising of this, that arises. When this does not exist, that does not come to be; with the cessation of this, that ceases.'

"'That is, with ignorance as condition, volitional activities come to be; with volitional activities as condition, consciousness. . . . Such is the origin of this whole mass of suffering. But with the remainderless fading away and cessation of ignorance there is cessation of volitional activities; with the cessation of volitional activities, cessation of consciousness. . . . Such is the cessation of this whole mass of suffering.' This is the noble method that he has well seen and well penetrated with wisdom.

"When, householder, these five perils and enemies have subsided in a noble disciple, and he possesses these four factors of stream-entry and has well seen and well penetrated with wisdom this noble method, if he wishes he could by himself declare himself thus: 'I am one finished with hell, finished with the animal realm, finished with the domain of spirits, finished with the plane of misery, the bad destinations, the lower world. I am a stream-enterer, no longer subject to the lower world, fixed [in destiny], with enlightenment as destination.'"

8. *Parivīmaṃsanasutta*
Investigation (SN 12:51; II 80–84)

[1. The investigation]
"Here, monks, when investigating, a monk investigates thus: 'The manifold different kinds of suffering that arise in the world [headed by] old-age-and-death: what is the cause of this suffering, what is its origin, what is its genesis, what is its source? When what exists does old-age-and-death come to be? When what does not exist does old-age-and-death not come to be?'

"As he investigates, he understands thus: 'The manifold different kinds of suffering that arise in the world [headed by] old-age-and-death: this suffering has birth as its cause, birth as its origin, birth as its genesis, birth as its source. When there is birth, old-age-and-death comes to be; when there is no birth, old-age-and-death does not come to be.'

"He understands old-age-and-death, its origin, its cessation, and the way going in conformity with its cessation.[63] He practices in that way and acts in accordance with the Dhamma. This is called a monk who is practicing for the entirely complete destruction of suffering, for the cessation of old-age-and-death.

"Then, further investigating, he investigates thus: 'What is the cause of this birth?. . . What is the cause of this existence? . . . What is the cause of this clinging?. . . What is the cause of this craving?. . . What is the cause of this feeling?. . . What is the cause of this contact?. . . What is the cause of these six sense bases?. . . What is the cause of this name-and-form? . . . What is the cause of this consciousness?. . . What is the cause of these volitional activities, what is their origin, what is their genesis, what is their source? When what exists do volitional activities come to be? When what does not exist do volitional activities not come to be?'

"As he investigates, he understands thus: 'Volitional activities have ignorance as their cause, ignorance as their origin, ignorance as their genesis, ignorance as their source. When there is ignorance, volitional activities come to be; when there is no ignorance, volitional activities do not come to be.'

"He understands volitional activities, their origin, their cessation, and the way going in conformity with their cessation. He practices in that way and acts in accordance with the Dhamma. This is called a monk who is practicing for the entirely complete destruction of suffering, for the cessation of volitional activities.

[2. Liberation]

"If, monks, this ignorant person generates a meritorious volitional activity, consciousness approaches the meritorious. If he generates a demeritorious volitional activity, consciousness approaches the demeritorious. If he generates an imperturbable volitional activity, consciousness approaches the imperturbable.[64]

"But when a monk has abandoned ignorance and given rise to clear knowledge, then, with the fading away of ignorance and the arising of clear knowledge, he does not generate a meritorious volitional activity, or a demeritorious volitional activity, or an imperturbable volitional activity.

"One not generating or producing [any volitional activities] does not cling to anything in the world. Not clinging, he does not thirst. Not thirsting, he personally attains nibbāna. He understands: 'Finished is birth, the spiritual life has been lived, what had to be done has been done, there is no further for this state of being.'

[3. Nibbāna with residue][65]

"If he feels a pleasant feeling, he understands: 'It's impermanent'; he understands: 'It's not held to'; he understands: 'It's not delighted in.' If he feels a painful feeling, he understands: 'It's impermanent'; he understands: 'It's not held to'; he understands: 'It's not delighted in.' If he feels a neither-painful-nor-pleasant feeling, he understands: 'It's impermanent'; he understands: 'It's not held to'; he understands: 'It's not delighted in.' If he feels a pleasant feeling, he feels it detached; if he feels a painful feeling, he feels it detached; if he feels a neither-painful-nor-pleasant feeling, he feels it detached.

"When he feels a feeling limited by the body, he understands: 'I feel a feeling limited by the body.' When he feels a feeling limited by life, he understands: 'I feel a feeling limited by life.'[66] He understands: 'With the breakup of the body, following the exhaustion of life, all that is felt, not being delighted in, will become cool right here; bodily remnants will remain.'

"Suppose, monks, a man would remove a hot clay pot from a potter's oven and set it down on even ground. Its heat would subside right there and shards would remain. So too, when he feels a feeling limited by the body, he understands: 'I feel a feeling limited by the body.' When he feels a feeling limited by life, he understands: 'I feel a feeling limited by life.' He understands: 'With the breakup of the body, following the exhaustion of life, all that is felt, not being delighted in, will become cool right here; bodily remnants will remain.'

[4. Nibbāna without residue]
"What do you think, monks? Would a monk whose influxes are destroyed generate a meritorious volitional activity, or a demeritorious volitional activity, or an imperturbable volitional activity?"—"Surely not, Bhante."—"When volitional activities are completely absent, with the cessation of volitional activities, would consciousness be discerned?"—"Surely not, Bhante."

"When consciousness is completely absent, with the cessation of consciousness, would name-and-form be discerned?"—"Surely not, Bhante."—"When name-and-form is completely absent. . . . When the six sense bases are completely absent. . . . When contact is completely absent. . . . When feeling is completely absent. . . . When craving is completely absent. . . . When clinging is completely absent. . . . When existence is completely absent, with the cessation of existence, would birth be discerned?"—"Surely not, Bhante."—"When birth is completely absent, with the cessation of birth, would old-age-and-death be discerned?"—"Surely not, Bhante."

"Good, good, monks! So it is, and not otherwise. Have faith in me about that, monks, be convinced. Be without perplexity about this, without doubt. This itself is the end of suffering."[67]

9. *Mahārukkhasutta*
The Great Tree (SN 12:55; II 87–88)

"Monks, if one dwells contemplating enjoyment in things that can be clung to, craving increases.[68] With craving as condition, clinging occurs; with clinging as condition, existence. . . . Such is the origin of this whole mass of suffering.

"Suppose, monks, there were a great tree. Its downward-going roots and those going across would all convey the sap upward. Thus that great tree, with that sap as nutriment, with that sap as sustenance, would stand for a very long time. Just so, monks, if one dwells contemplating enjoyment in things that can be clung to, craving increases. With craving as condition, clinging occurs. . . . Such is the origin of this whole mass of suffering.

"But, monks, if one dwells contemplating danger in things that can be clung to, craving ceases. With the cessation of craving there is cessation of clinging; with the cessation of clinging, cessation of existence. . . . Such is the cessation of this whole mass of suffering.

"Suppose, monks, there were a great tree. Then a person would come with a shovel and a basket. He would cut that tree at the root, dig around it, and pull up the roots, even those the size of *usīra* fibers. He would cut that tree into pieces, split the pieces, and reduce them to splinters. Having made splinters, he would dry them in the wind and the sun's heat, burn them with fire, and make ashes. Having made ashes, he would winnow them in a strong wind or have them carried off by a river with a swift current. Thus indeed, monks, that great tree would be cut off at the root, made like a palm stump, obliterated, not subject to future arising.

"Just so, monks, if one dwells contemplating danger in things that can be clung to, craving ceases. With the cessation of craving there is cessation of clinging; with the cessation of clinging, cessation of existence. . . . Such is the cessation of this whole mass of suffering."

10. *Assutavāsutta*
Unlearned (SN 12:61; II 94–95)

[1. The worldling grasps the mind]
"The unlearned worldling, monks, might become disenchanted with this physical body,[69] might become dispassionate toward it and be liberated from it. For what reason? Because there is seen in this physical body growth and decline, taking up and putting down. Therefore the unlearned worldling might become disenchanted with this physical body, might become dispassionate toward it and be liberated from it.

"But, monks, as to that which is called 'mind' and 'thought' and 'consciousness'[70]—the unlearned worldling is unable to become disenchanted with it, unable to become dispassionate toward it, unable to be liberated from it. For what reason? Because, monks, for a long time the unlearned worldling has held this, appropriated it, and grasped it thus: 'This is mine, this I am, this is my self.' Therefore the unlearned worldling is unable to become disenchanted with it, unable to become dispassionate toward it, unable to be liberated from it.

[2. Better to grasp the body than the mind]
"It would be better, monks, for the unlearned worldling to take this physical body as self rather than the mind. For what reason? Because this physical body is seen standing for one year, for two years, for three, four, five, or ten years, for twenty, thirty, forty, or fifty years, for a hundred years, or even more.

"But that which is called 'mind' and 'thought' and 'consciousness,' by day and by night, arises as one thing and ceases as another. Just as a monkey roaming in a forest grove grabs hold of one branch, releases it and grabs another, then releases it and grabs still another, so too that which is called 'mind' and 'thought' and 'consciousness,' by day and by night, arises as one thing and ceases as another.

[3. Contemplating dependent origination]
"In regard to that, monks, the learned noble disciple well attends thoroughly to dependent origination thus: 'When this exists, that comes to be; with the arising of this, that arises. When this does not exist, that does not come to be; with the

cessation of this, that ceases—that is, with ignorance as condition, volitional activities come to be; with volitional activities as condition, consciousness. . . . Such is the origin of this whole mass of suffering. But with the remainderless fading away and cessation of ignorance there is cessation of volitional activities; with the cessation of volitional activities, cessation of consciousness. . . . Such is the cessation of this whole mass of suffering.'

"Seeing thus, the learned noble disciple becomes disenchanted with form, disenchanted with feeling, disenchanted with perception, disenchanted with volitional activities, disenchanted with consciousness. Being disenchanted, he becomes dispassionate. Through dispassion he is liberated. In regard to what is liberated, the knowledge occurs thus: 'Liberated.' He understands: 'Finished is birth, the spiritual life has been lived, what had to be done has been done, there is no further for this state of being.'"

11. *Nagarasutta*
The City (SN 12:65; II 104–7)

[1. Discovering the path to enlightenment]
"Before the enlightenment, monks, while I was just a bodhisatta, not fully enlightened, this occurred to me: 'Alas, this world has fallen into trouble; it is born, grows old, and dies, it passes away and is reborn, yet it does not understand the escape from this suffering, from old-age-and-death. When now will an escape be discerned from this suffering, from old-age-and-death?'[71]

"Then, monks, this occurred to me: 'When what exists does old-age-and-death come to be? By what is old-age-and-death conditioned?' Then, through thorough attention, there took place in me a breakthrough by wisdom: 'When there is birth, old-age-and-death occurs; with birth as condition, there is old-age-and-death.'

"Then, monks, this occurred to me: 'When what exists does birth come to be . . . existence . . . clinging . . . craving . . . feeling . . . contact . . . the six sense bases . . . name-and-form come to be? By what is name-and-form conditioned?' Then, through thorough attention, there took place in me a breakthrough by wisdom: 'When there is consciousness, name-and-form comes to be; with consciousness as condition, there is name-and-form.'

"Then, monks, this occurred to me: 'When what exists does consciousness come to be? By what is consciousness conditioned?' Then, through thorough attention, there took place in me a breakthrough by wisdom: 'When there is name-and-form, consciousness comes to be; with consciousness as condition there is name-and-form.'[72]

"Then, monks, this occurred to me: 'This consciousness turns back; it does not go further than name-and-form. It is to this extent that one may be born and grow old and die, pass away and be reborn—that is, when there is consciousness with name-and-form as its condition, and name-and-form with consciousness as its condition. With name-and-form as condition, the six sense bases come to be; with the six sense bases as condition, contact. . . . Such is the origin of this whole mass of suffering.'

"'Origin, origin'—thus, monks, in regard to things unheard before, the eye arose in me, knowledge arose, wisdom arose, clear knowledge arose, light arose.

"Then, monks, this occurred to me: 'When what does not exist does old-age-and-death not come to be? With the cessation of what is there cessation of old-age-and-death?' Then, through thorough attention, there took place in me a breakthrough by wisdom: 'When there is no birth, old-age-and-death does not come to be; with the cessation of birth there is cessation of old-age-and-death.'

"Then, monks, this occurred to me: 'When what does not exist does birth not come to be . . . existence . . . clinging . . . craving . . . feeling . . . contact . . . the six sense bases . . . name-and-form not come to be? With the cessation of what is there cessation of name-and-form?' Then, through thorough attention, there took place in me a breakthrough by wisdom: 'When there is no consciousness, name-and-form does not come to be; with the cessation of consciousness there is cessation of name-and-form.'

"Then, monks, this occurred to me: 'When what does not exist does consciousness not come to be? With the cessation of what is there cessation of consciousness?' Then, through thorough attention, there took place in me a breakthrough by wisdom: 'When there is no name-and-form, consciousness does not come to be; with the cessation of name-and-form there is cessation of consciousness.'

"This occurred to me, monks: 'I have discovered this path to enlightenment—that is, with the cessation of name-and-form there is cessation of consciousness; with the cessation of consciousness there is cessation of name-and-form. With the cessation of name-and-form, cessation of the six sense bases; with the cessation of the six sense bases, cessation of contact. . . . Such is the cessation of this whole mass of suffering.'

"'Cessation, cessation'—thus, monks, for me, in regard to things unheard before, the eye arose in me, knowledge arose, wisdom arose, clear knowledge arose, light arose.

[2. The simile of the city]

"Suppose, monks, a man wandering in a forest grove would see an ancient path, an ancient road, traveled along by people in the past. He would follow it and would see an ancient city, an ancient capital, inhabited by people in the past, possessing parks, groves, ponds, and mounds, delightful.

"Then the man would report to the king or to the king's chief minister: 'Sire, you should know that while wandering through a forest grove I saw an ancient path, an ancient road, traveled along by people in the past. I followed it and saw an ancient city, an ancient capital, inhabited by people in the past, possessing parks, groves, ponds, and mounds, delightful. Renovate that city, sire!'

"Then, monks, that king or the king's chief minister would renovate that city. Some time later that city would become successful and prosperous, populated, filled with people, attained to growth and expansion.

"So too, monks, I saw the ancient path, the ancient road, traveled along by the perfectly enlightened ones of the past. And what is that ancient path, that ancient road? It is just this noble eightfold path—that is, right view . . . right concentration. This is the ancient path, the ancient road, traveled along by the perfectly enlightened ones of the past.

"I followed it and have directly known old-age-and-death, its origin, its cessation, and the way leading to its cessation. I followed it and have directly known birth . . . existence . . .

clinging . . . craving . . . feeling . . . contact . . . the six sense bases . . . name-and-form . . . consciousness . . . volitional activities, their origin, their cessation, and the way leading to their cessation.

"Having directly known that, I have pointed that out to the monks, the nuns, the male lay followers, and the female lay followers. This spiritual life, monks, has become successful and prosperous, extensive, popular, widespread, well proclaimed among devas and humans."

12. *Sammasanasutta*
Exploration (SN 12:66; II 107–12)

[1. Inward exploration]
Thus have I heard. On one occasion the Blessed One was dwelling among the Kurus, where there was a town of the Kurus named Kammāsadamma. There the Blessed One addressed the monks: "Monks!"—"Venerable one!" those monks replied. The Blessed One said this: "Do you, monks, engage in inward exploration?" When this was said, a certain monk said to the Blessed One: "Bhante, I engage in inward exploration."

"But how, monk, do you engage in inward exploration?" The monk then explained, but his explanation did not satisfy the Blessed One. Then the Venerable Ānanda said this to the Blessed One: "Now is the time for this, Blessed One! Now is the time for this, Fortunate One! Let the Blessed One speak of inward exploration. Having heard it from the Blessed One, the monks will retain it in mind."—"In that case, Ānanda, listen and attend well. I will speak."—"Yes, Bhante," those monks replied. The Blessed One said this:

"Here, monks, when engaged in inward exploration, a monk explores thus: 'The manifold different kinds of suffering that arise in the world [headed by] old-age-and-death: what is the cause of this suffering, what is its origin, what is its genesis, what is its source? When what exists does old-age-and-death come to be? When what does not exist does old-age-and-death not come to be?'

"As he is exploring, he knows thus: 'The manifold different kinds of suffering that arise in the world [headed by] old-age-and-death: this suffering has acquisition as its cause, acquisition as its origin, acquisition as its genesis, acquisition as its source.[73] When there is acquisition, old-age-and-death comes to be; when there is no acquisition, old-age-and-death does not come to be.'

"He understands old-age-and-death, its origin, its cessation, and the way going in conformity with its cessation. He practices in that way and acts in accordance with the Dhamma. This is called a monk who is practicing for the entirely complete destruction of suffering, for the cessation of old-age-and-death.

"Then, engaging further in inward exploration, he explores thus: 'What is the cause of this acquisition, what is its origin, what is its genesis, what is its source? When what exists does acquisition come to be; when what does not exist does acquisition not come to be?'

"As he is exploring, he knows thus: 'Acquisition has craving as its cause, craving as its origin, craving as its genesis, craving as its source. When there is craving, acquisition comes to be; when there is no craving, acquisition does not come to be.'

"He understands acquisition, its origin, its cessation, and the way going in conformity with its cessation. He practices in that way and acts in accordance with the Dhamma. This is called a monk who is practicing for the entirely complete destruction of suffering, for the cessation of acquisition.

"Then, engaging further in inward exploration, he explores thus: 'Where does this craving arise? Where does it settle down?'

"As he explores, he understands thus: 'Whatever in the world has a pleasant and agreeable nature: here this craving arises; here it settles down.'

"And what in the world has a pleasant and agreeable nature? The eye has a pleasant and agreeable nature; here this craving arises; here it settles down. The ear has a pleasant and agreeable nature. . . . The nose has a pleasant and agreeable nature. . . . The tongue has a pleasant and agreeable nature. . . . The body has a pleasant and agreeable nature. . . . The mind has a pleasant and agreeable nature; here this craving arises; here it settles down.

[2. Those not freed from suffering]

"Monks, whatever ascetics and brahmins in the past regarded

things in the world that have a pleasant and agreeable nature as permanent, as happiness, as self, as healthy, as secure: they increased craving. Those who increased craving increased acquisition. Those who increased acquisition increased suffering. Those who increased suffering were not freed from birth, old age, and death, from sorrow, lamentation, pain, dejection, and misery. 'They were not freed from suffering,' I say.

"Whatever ascetics and brahmins in the future, too, will regard things in the world that have a pleasant and agreeable nature as permanent, as happiness, as self, as healthy, as secure: they will increase craving. Those who will increase craving will increase acquisition. Those who will increase acquisition will increase suffering. Those who will increase suffering will not be freed from birth, old age, and death, from sorrow, lamentation, pain, dejection, and misery. 'They will not be freed from suffering,' I say.

"Whatever ascetics and brahmins at present, too, regard things in the world that have a pleasant and agreeable nature as permanent, as happiness, as self, as healthy, as secure: they increase craving. Those who increase craving increase acquisition. Those who increase acquisition increase suffering. Those who increase suffering are not freed from birth, old age, and death, from sorrow, lamentation, pain, dejection, and misery. 'They are not freed from suffering,' I say.

"Suppose, monks, there was a beverage having a fine color, fragrance, and flavor, but it was mixed with poison. Then a man would come along, oppressed and afflicted by the heat, tired, thirsty, and parched. They would tell him: 'Good man, this beverage has a fine color, fragrance, and flavor, but it is mixed with poison. Drink it if you wish. If you drink it, you will be pleased with its color, fragrance, and flavor, but on that account you will undergo death or deadly suffering.' Suddenly, unreflectively, he would drink the beverage—he would not relinquish it—and on that account he would undergo death or deadly suffering.

"So too, monks, whatever ascetics and brahmins in the past . . . in the future . . . at present regard things in the world that have a pleasant and agreeable nature as permanent, as happiness, as self, as healthy, as secure: they increase craving. Those who increase craving increase acquisition. Those who increase acquisition increase suffering. Those who increase suffering are not freed from birth, old age, and death, from sorrow, lamentation, pain, dejection, and misery. 'They are not freed from suffering,' I say.

[3. Those freed from suffering]
"But, monks, whatever ascetics and brahmins in the past regarded things in the world that have a pleasant and agreeable nature as impermanent, as suffering, as non-self, as an illness, as perilous: they abandoned craving. Those who abandoned craving abandoned acquisition. Those who abandoned acquisition abandoned suffering. Those who abandoned suffering were freed from birth, old age, and death, from sorrow, lamentation, pain, dejection, and misery. 'They were freed from suffering,' I say.

"Whatever ascetics and brahmins in the future, too, will regard things in the world that have a pleasant and agreeable nature as impermanent, as suffering, as non-self, as an illness, as perilous: they will abandon craving. Those who will abandon craving . . . 'They will be freed from suffering,' I say.

"Whatever ascetics and brahmins at present, too, regard things in the world that have a pleasant and agreeable nature as impermanent, as suffering, as non-self, as an illness, as perilous: they abandon craving. Those who abandon craving . . . 'They are freed from suffering,' I say.

"Suppose, monks, there was a beverage having a fine color, fragrance, and flavor, but it was mixed with poison. Then a man would come along, oppressed and afflicted by the heat, tired, thirsty, and parched. They would tell him: 'Good man, this beverage has a fine color, fragrance, and flavor, but it is mixed with poison. Drink it if you wish. If you drink it, you will be pleased with its color, fragrance, and flavor, but on that account you will undergo death or deadly suffering.'

"Then it would occur to that man: 'I can quench my thirst with water, whey, porridge, or soup, but I should not drink that beverage, which would lead to my harm and suffering for a long time.' Having reflected, he would not drink the beverage but would relinquish it, and on that account he would not undergo death or deadly suffering.

"So too, monks, whatever ascetics and brahmins in the past . . . whatever ascetics and brahmins in the future . . . whatever ascetics and brahmins at present regard things in the world that have a pleasant and agreeable nature as impermanent, as suffering, as non-self, as an illness, as perilous: they abandon craving. Those who abandon craving abandon acquisition. Those who abandon acquisition abandon suffering. Those who abandon suffering are freed from birth, from old age, from death, from sorrow, lamentation, pain, dejection, and misery. 'They are freed from suffering,' I say."

5. The Path and the Way: The Practices Leading to the End of Suffering

Introduction

Since ignorance and craving are the underlying roots of dukkha, it follows that to reach the cessation of dukkha, ignorance and craving must be extricated. To remove them is the task of the path. In his first discourse, the Buddha described the noble eightfold path as "the way to the cessation of suffering." However, while the noble eightfold path is the best-known program of practice for reaching the end of dukkha, the suttas offer various sets of factors, partly corresponding to the eightfold path, as alternative formulations of the way to the attainment of the goal.

These are grouped into seven sets comprising a total of thirty-seven constituents:

- the four establishments of mindfulness (*cattāro satipaṭṭhānā*)
- the four right kinds of striving (*cattāro sammappadhānā*)
- the four bases for spiritual potency (*cattāro iddhipādā*)
- the five faculties (*pañc'indriyāni*)
- the five powers (*pañca balāni*)
- the seven factors of enlightenment (*satta bojjhaṅgā*)
- the noble eightfold path (*ariya aṭṭhaṅgika magga*)

The seven sets are closely interwoven, and thus a single factor may appear multiple times among different groups in the list. Mindfulness, for instance, appears in the four establishments of mindfulness; again as a faculty, power, and factor of enlightenment; and still again as right mindfulness in the eightfold path. Energy appears as the four right strivings; as a basis for spiritual potency; as a faculty, power, and enlightenment factor; and as right effort in the eightfold path. Concentration and wisdom, too, appear in several sets, the latter under different designations: as investigation (*vīmaṃsā*) among the bases for spiritual potency, as discrimination of phenomena (*dhammavicaya*) among the enlightenment factors, and as right view (*sammādiṭṭhi*) in the noble eightfold path.

The different sets were probably designed to meet the aptitudes and inclinations of different practitioners. The Mahāvagga, the last volume of the Saṃyutta Nikāya, contains separate chapters on each of these groups. Since including suttas from each group would have increased the present chapter to excessive size, I have selected suttas from only three groups, taking them as sufficiently representative of the entire collection. I have also changed the order of presentation, in effect inverting the order in which they appear in the Mahāvagga. I place the four establishments of mindfulness first, taking it to be the fundamental contemplative practice. I follow these with the seven factors of enlightenment, and these with the noble eightfold path.

This change can be justified by the fact that mindfulness—developed through the four establishments of mindfulness—serves as the first enlightenment factor, from which the other six factors of enlightenment emerge, culminating in the enlightenment factor of equanimity. The seven factors of enlightenment might be seen either as engendering the world-transcending noble eightfold path or as an alternative course of development complementary to and partly overlapping the eightfold path.

Before describing these groups individually, I must caution against a common misunderstanding. It is often assumed that the thirty-seven aids to enlightenment—particularly the noble eightfold path—encompass the entirety of Buddhist practice, that all the guidelines to well-being taught by the Buddha can fit into this framework. This, however, is not the case. The thirty-seven aids are the set of factors needed to reach the ultimate goal of the Dhamma, the supreme good among the three aims of the teaching (see p. 2). They are the practices that "lead to going from the near shore to the far shore" (*apārā pāraṃ gamanāya saṃvattanti*, SN 45:34), but the Buddha offered many practices conducive to happiness and well-being for those content to remain dwelling on "the near shore," who seek the temporal good rather than the final good. These include the qualities extolled in the Maṅgala Sutta (Sn 265–69) such as generosity, reverence, humility, contentment, gratitude, and patience. They include practices rooted in faith and devotion, such as the six recollections (see AN 6:10; AN 6:25). And they include the four immeasurable states and the four means of sustaining a wholesome relationship.[74] All these qualities and virtues can be regarded as the basis for moral and psychological well-being and as the prerequisites for world-transcending realization, but on their own they are not sufficient to bring the attainment of the supreme goal. That requires the concerted power of tranquility and insight, concentration and wisdom, which emerge by developing the thirty-seven aids to enlightenment.

The four establishments of mindfulness

The primary textual source for the four establishments of mindfulness is the *Satipaṭṭhāna Sutta*, which occurs twice in the Nikāyas: in a more concise version as MN 10 (probably more original) and in an expanded version as DN 22. The latter differs from the former only in providing detailed definitions of the four noble truths.

The expression *satipaṭṭhāna* is usually rendered "foundation of mindfulness," on the supposition that the compound is formed from *sati*, "mindfulness," and *paṭṭhāna*, understood as a basis or support, hence "foundation." However, while this interpretation is possible, the term is more likely to be a compound of *sati* and *upaṭṭhāna*, "setting up" or "establishing." In such a case, the rendering "establishment of mindfulness," which I have adopted, would be more accurate.

The four *satipaṭṭhāna* are contemplation of the body, contemplation of feelings, contemplation of mind, and contemplation of *dhammas*, a word I render somewhat inadequately as "phenomena." Since the suttas in the Satipaṭṭhānasaṃyutta do not explain the four establishments of mindfulness, a brief overview of this fourfold scheme, based on the *Satipaṭṭhāna Sutta*, is warranted here.

Of the four contemplations, the contemplation of the body is concerned with the material side of existence, the middle two with the mental side, and the last with the exploration of experience from a variety of angles, all oriented toward the goal of the teaching. The four unfold in a definite sequence. Starting with the body as the coarsest, they proceed through contemplation of feelings and the mind and culminate in the last, contemplation of phenomena, which is the subtlest.

Contemplation of the body (*kāyānupassanā*) is said to comprise fourteen exercises, but since the last nine are mere variations on a single theme, these effectively amount to six. The first is *mindfulness of breathing*. To undertake this practice, one puts the natural process of breathing under the lens of mindful observation. Breathing naturally, one focuses on the breath, distinguishing the two phases of breathing in and breathing out. The key to the entire practice is succinctly expressed in the Buddha's statement: "Just mindful one breathes in, mindful one breathes out." The awareness of breath cuts through the complexities of discursive thinking, pulling the mind back from its habitual meandering and anchoring it in the present. As the practice advances, one distinguishes whether the breath is long or short; then one experiences the entire body while mindfully breathing in and out; and then one calms the bodily processes while mindfully breathing in and out.

The next exercise is *mindfulness of the postures*, which extends mindfulness to all postures: walking, standing, sitting, and lying down, and to the change from one posture to another. Contemplation of the postures illuminates the impersonal nature of the body, revealing it to be a configuration of living matter subject to the directing influence of volition.

The next exercise, called *mindfulness and clear comprehension*, applies mindfulness to the diverse activities of daily life. Clear comprehension is mentioned in relation to all four *satipaṭṭhāna*, where it serves as an inseparable companion to mindfulness, but it is sometimes singled out as a distinct practice in its own right, as in **5.1.2**. In such cases, it is said that one should bring clear comprehension to bear on the familiar activities of daily life: walking, looking around, bending and stretching the limbs, dressing, eating, speaking, going to the toilet, and so forth. We might suppose that in the meditative development of mindfulness, clear comprehension is ever-present in a background role, while in performing the tasks of daily life, clear comprehension steps up to the forefront, with mindfulness now relegated to a supporting role.

The next two exercises are analytical contemplations of the body's real nature. The first is the meditation on *the body's impurity*, proposed as the direct antidote to sensual lust. In this exercise, one contemplates the body's anatomical constitution, mentally dissecting one's body into its components to bring to light their unattractive nature. The sutta mentions thirty-one bodily parts, which include various organs, tissues, and bodily fluids. In later versions, the number is increased to thirty-two with the addition of the brain.

The other analytical contemplation is meditation on *the four physical elements*, designed to counter the innate tendency to identify with the body and take it as "I" and "mine." The exercise proceeds by mentally dissecting the body into the four primary elements, referred to as earth, water, fire, and air. Having analyzed the body into the four elements, one then considers all the elements to be essentially identical with their external counterparts. This exposes the body's impersonal nature and removes the ground for taking the body as "I" and "mine."

The last exercise in mindfulness of the body is a series of nine *charnel ground contemplations*, meditations on the body's disintegration after death. Since it is hard these days to observe bodily disintegration firsthand, this can be practiced imaginatively or with the aid of pictures. The aim of this exercise is not to incite a morbid fascination with death and corpses but to sunder our instinctive clinging to the body by revealing its inexorable transience.

The second establishment of mindfulness is contemplation of feeling (*vedanānupassanā*), where the word "feeling" does not refer to emotion but to the bare affective tone of experience, whether pleasant, painful, or neutral. Feeling is of special importance as an object of contemplation because it serves as fodder for the latent defilements. Pleasant feeling nourishes greed and attachment, painful feeling provokes aversion, and neutral feeling sustains delusion, which manifests as apathy and complacency. The link between feelings and the defilements is not inevitable but can be severed by bringing arisen feelings into the range of mindfulness and seeing into their transient nature, the task of wisdom.

The third establishment of mindfulness is contemplation of mind (*cittānupassanā*), which entails observing arisen states of mind. Under this contemplation, the Buddha mentions sixteen mental states grouped in eight pairs: the mind with lust and without lust; with aversion and without aversion; with delusion and without delusion; the cramped mind and the scattered mind; the developed mind and the undeveloped mind; the surpassable mind and the unsurpassable mind; the concentrated mind and the unconcentrated mind; and the freed mind and the bound mind. Again, seeing the uninterrupted change of mental states brings to light the impermanence of the mind.

The final establishment of mindfulness is contemplation of phenomena (*dhammānupassanā*), the most complex and diverse of the four bases of mindfulness. Here the word *dhamma* refers to groups of phenomena organized in ways that reflect the movement and goal of the Buddha's teaching. The five groups mentioned are: the five hindrances, the five aggregates, the six pairs of sense bases, the seven factors of enlightenment, and the four noble truths. The five hindrances are the obstacles to realization, while the seven factors of enlightenment are the qualities that conduce to realization. The aggregates and sense bases offer different takes on the phenomenological field, which is to be explored with insight, while the four noble truths constitute the sphere of realization itself.

One first overcomes the five hindrances. Once the hindrances are out of the way, one embarks on the contemplation of experience, doing so from either of two perspectives: by way of the five aggregates or the six pairs of internal and external sense bases. Through this contemplation the seven factors of enlightenment arise and gain in strength. When the seven factors reach maturity, they blossom in the direct realization of the *four noble truths*: the truths of suffering, its origin, its cessation, and the path. It is this realization that permanently uproots the defilements and brings liberation from dukkha.

In **5.1.1**, as in the *Satipaṭṭhāna Sutta*, the Buddha describes the four establishments of mindfulness as *ekāyana magga*. The expression has sometimes been rendered "the only way" or "the sole way," but it seems unlikely that this was the original meaning. Literally, the expression means "one-going path" or "one-way path." I take this to mean a path going in one direction—that is, heading directly toward the destinations that follow, from "the purification of beings" through "the realization of nibbāna." The dative case, which can signify the goal of movement, is used for these expressions in the opening declaration, and this may be cited as support for my interpretation.

The formula describing the practice shows that the practitioner must not only be mindful but also "ardent" (*ātāpī*), which represents the factor of energy or effort, and "clearly comprehending" (*sampajāno*), which suggests emergent wisdom. For the endeavor to succeed, moreover, one must also remove—or be intent on removing—"longing and dejection" in regard to worldly conditions. These states correspond roughly to the first two of the five hindrances, and thus their removal points to the emergence of concentration.

The cultivation of mindfulness is almost invariably coupled with *sampajañña*, which I render as "clear comprehension." Others have rendered this term as "full awareness" or "alertness." The word is based on the root *ñā*, meaning "to know," with two prefixes, *sam-* and *pa-*. While a separate exercise emphasizing clear comprehension is included under contemplation of the body, this factor enters into each of the four contemplations and is thus an invariable part of the practice. The standard formula for the establishments of mindfulness says that the meditator engaging in each of the four contemplations should be "clearly comprehending" (*sampajāno*), which entails that clear comprehension is integral to the entire process initiated by mindfulness.

The suttas selected for this chapter do not provide a detailed explanation of the four establishments of mindfulness but rather highlight different contexts for the practice. Thus **5.1.3** states that the four are to be adopted by monastics at different stages of maturity—novices, trainees, and arahants—each for a different purpose. It is significant that in the first two cases the cultivation of mindfulness contributes to the arising of insight or understanding; it does not pertain merely to the development of concentration, as is sometimes claimed. In **5.1.5** we encounter the story of the Buddha's grave illness, a narrative also found in the *Mahāparinibbāna Sutta* (DN 16, at II 98–101). Aware that his end was drawing near, he suppressed the illness and instructed the monks to be islands and refuges for themselves, which they can do by practicing the four establishments of mindfulness. Text **5.1.8** shows that the four establishments of mindfulness should be cultivated even in times of illness; the subject of the discourse is a layman who at the end proclaims himself a non-returner. Several suttas offer memorable similes: the monkey that wanders outside its own domain and gets stuck in hunter's glue (**5.1.4**); the acrobats who protect each other by protecting themselves (**5.1.6**); and the man ordered to carry a bowl of oil through a boisterous crowd under threat of decapitation (**5.1.7**).

The seven factors of enlightenment

Properly cultivated, the four establishments of mindfulness naturally give rise to the seven factors of enlightenment, which begin with the factor of mindfulness. The standard formula for the enlightenment factors says, with regard to each, that it is "based on seclusion, based on dispassion, based on cessation, evolving toward relinquishment."[75] We might see the terms "seclusion, dispassion, and cessation" as representing the goal toward which one aspires when undertaking the practice, and "evolving toward relinquishment" as indicating the inherent capacity of these factors to culminate in that goal.

In **5.2.4** the Buddha explains that these seven factors of enlightenment are so called because they lead to enlightenment. While this seems obvious, the explanation is noteworthy because the commentarial tradition takes the seven *bojjhaṅgā* to be primarily *constituents* of the enlightenment experience rather than factors leading to enlightenment, Here, however, they are said to be the qualities that lead to enlightenment.

This interpretation is confirmed by **5.2.3**, which shows how the seven factors unfold in a graded sequence, each one coming to prominence when its predecessor reaches a sufficient degree of strength. Text **5.2.5** again highlights the instrumental role of the enlightenment factors as well as their place in the sequential development of the practice. The seven factors culminate in "clear knowledge and liberation"; they do not constitute clear knowledge as such. The seven factors in turn arise through the development of the four establishments of mindfulness, which depend on the three kinds of good conduct, which in turn require the exercise of sense restraint.

The seven factors of enlightenment are sometimes paired in an antithetical relationship with the five hindrances, the obstacles to progress. Text **5.2.2** first explains the "nutriments" for the five hindrances, which are to be overcome by "starving" them; it then explains the nutriments for the seven factors of enlightenment, the things that properly nourish them. Although it is not expressly mentioned in the suttas, this positing of a conditional relationship between the two sets and their respective nutriments illustrates another application of the principle of conditionality that underlies dependent origination. By understanding how the hindrances arise and thrive through their nutriments, one knows how to remove them by withdrawing their sustaining conditions. By understanding how the enlightenment factors grow and flourish through their nutriments, one knows how to strengthen them and bring them to fulfillment.

This point is reinforced by **5.2.7**, which clarifies the kinds of skills required in cultivating the seven enlightenment factors. The seven factors are here divided into two groups—three arousing factors and three calming factors. As shown by the simile of kindling and extinguishing a fire, a proficient meditator must know the right occasions for developing the appropriate factors. There are occasions when the arousing factors should be cultivated but not the calming factors; and there are other occasions when the calming factors should be cultivated but not the arousing factors. Mindfulness, however, does not fall into either group for, as the text says, it is useful everywhere.

The noble eightfold path

The third division of this chapter introduces the noble eightfold path. Here, **5.3.3** provides formal definitions of the individual path factors. From these definitions, it can be seen that the path has a wider scope than the seven factors of enlightenment.

Whereas the latter scheme operates almost entirely in the domain of meditative practice, the eightfold path includes a cognitive factor, right view; a motivational factor, right intention; and three ethical factors: right speech, right action, and right livelihood. These all precede and support the three meditative factors—right effort, right mindfulness, and right concentration—though when the path comes to maturity, all eight operate in unison.

The suttas of the Maggasaṃyutta attach two alternative descriptions to each path factor. One is the "based on seclusion" formula also used in relation to the enlightenment factors. The other describes each path factor as "culminating in the removal of lust, the removal of hatred, the removal of delusion."[76] Often in this compilation duplicate versions of a sutta appear, differing only in the description they attach to the path factors. One version describes the factors with the "based on seclusion" formula, the other version with the "removal of lust" formula. I have included instances of this duplication here in **5.3.5** and **5.3.6**.

Three suttas in this anthology connect the eightfold path to good friendship. In **5.3.1** the Buddha corrects Ānanda's assertion that half the spiritual life consists in good friendship, declaring that the entire spiritual life is good friendship. He goes on to say that he himself is the good friend of beings, one who helps to liberate them from birth, old age, and death. The two suttas combined in **5.3.5**, which differ only in the formula they attach to the path factors, state that good friendship is the forerunner of the noble eightfold path. The penultimate sutta included in this chapter, **5.3.7**, declares that just as the Ganges River, which flows to the east, cannot be made to flow to the west, so a monk who has taken up the noble eightfold path cannot be persuaded to give up the training and revert to ordinary life. With a sureness of direction like the Ganges, the eightfold path carries the ardent disciple irreversibly toward nibbāna.

This same theme is taken up in the final text in this chapter, a composite of the ten suttas making up the *Oghavagga*, which explains the purpose of cultivating the noble eightfold path to be the direct knowledge, full understanding, destruction, and abandoning of the different groups of defilements mentioned elsewhere in the Nikāyas.

1. The Four Establishments of Mindfulness

1. *Ambapālisutta*
Ambapālī (SN 47:1; V 141)

Thus have I heard. On one occasion the Blessed One was dwelling at Vesālī in Ambapālī's grove. There the Blessed One said this: "This, monks, is a path going in one direction, toward the purification of beings, toward the overcoming of sorrow and lamentation, toward the passing away of pain and dejection, toward the achievement of the method, toward the realization of nibbāna—that is, the four establishments of mindfulness.[77]

"What four? Here, a monk dwells contemplating the body in the body, ardent, clearly comprehending, mindful, having removed longing and dejection in regard to the world; he dwells contemplating feelings in feelings, ardent, clearly comprehending, mindful, having removed longing and dejection in regard to the world; he dwells contemplating the mind in the mind, ardent, clearly comprehending, mindful, having removed longing and dejection in regard to the world; he dwells contemplating phenomena in phenomena, ardent, clearly comprehending, mindful, having removed longing and dejection in regard to the world.

"This, monks, is the path going in one direction, toward the purification of beings, toward the overcoming of sorrow and lamentation, toward the passing away of pain and dejection, toward the achievement of the method, toward the realization of nibbāna—that is, the four establishments of mindfulness."

2. *Satisutta*
Mindfulness (SN 47:2; V 142)

"Monks, a monk should dwell mindful and clearly comprehending. This is our instruction to you. And how, monks, is a monk mindful? Here, a monk dwells contemplating the body in the body, ardent, clearly comprehending, mindful, having removed longing and dejection in regard to the world; he dwells contemplating feelings in feelings . . . contemplating the mind in the mind . . . contemplating phenomena in phenomena, ardent, clearly comprehending, mindful, having removed longing and dejection in regard to the world. Thus a monk is mindful.

"And how, monks, is a monk clearly comprehending? Here, in going out and returning, a monk is one who acts with clear comprehension; in looking ahead and looking aside, he is one who acts with clear comprehension; in bending and stretching, he is one who acts with clear comprehension; in wearing the cloak and robe and [holding] the bowl, he is one who acts with clear comprehension; in eating, drinking, chewing, and tasting, he is one who acts with clear comprehension; in defecation and urination, he is one who acts with clear comprehension; in going, in standing, in sitting, in going to sleep, in waking up, in speaking, in keeping silent, he is one who acts with clear comprehension. Thus a monk is one who acts with clear comprehension.

"Monks, a monk should dwell mindful and clearly comprehending. This is our instruction to you."

3. *Sālasutta*
At Sāla (SN 47:4; V 144–45)

[1. Juniors]
"Monks, those monks who are juniors, not long gone forth, recently come to this Dhamma and discipline, should be enjoined, settled, and established by you in the development of the four establishments of mindfulness.

"What four? 'Come, friends, dwell contemplating the body in the body, ardent, clearly comprehending, unified, with tranquil minds, concentrated, with one-pointed minds, for knowledge of the body as it really is. Dwell contemplating feelings in feelings, ardent, clearly comprehending, unified, with tranquil minds, concentrated, with one-pointed minds, for knowledge of feelings as they really are. Dwell contemplating the mind in the mind, ardent, clearly comprehending, unified, with tranquil minds, concentrated, with one-pointed minds, for knowledge of the mind as it really is. Dwell contemplating phenomena in phenomena, ardent, clearly comprehending, unified, with tranquil minds, concentrated, with one-pointed minds, for knowledge of phenomena as they really are.'

[2. Trainees]

"Monks, those monks who are trainees,[78] who have not reached their mind's ideal, who dwell yearning for unsurpassed security from the bonds, they too dwell contemplating the body in the body, ardent, clearly comprehending, unified, with tranquil minds, concentrated, with one-pointed minds, for full understanding of the body. They dwell contemplating feelings in feelings, ardent, clearly comprehending, unified, with tranquil minds, concentrated, with one-pointed minds, for full understanding of feelings. They dwell contemplating the mind in the mind, ardent, clearly comprehending, unified, with tranquil minds, concentrated, with one-pointed minds, for full understanding of the mind. They dwell contemplating phenomena in phenomena, ardent, clearly comprehending, unified, with tranquil minds, concentrated, with one-pointed minds, for full understanding of phenomena.

[3. Arahants]

"Monks, those monks who are arahants, whose influxes are destroyed, who have lived the spiritual life, done what had to be done, dropped the burden, reached their own good, fully destroyed the fetters of existence, and are completely liberated by final knowledge, they too dwell contemplating the body in the body, ardent, clearly comprehending, unified, with tranquil minds, concentrated, with one-pointed minds, detached from the body. They dwell contemplating feelings in feelings, ardent, clearly comprehending, unified, with tranquil minds, concentrated, with one-pointed minds, detached from feelings. They dwell contemplating the mind in the mind, ardent, clearly comprehending, unified, with tranquil minds, concentrated, with one-pointed minds, detached from the mind. They dwell contemplating phenomena in phenomena, ardent, clearly comprehending, unified, with tranquil minds, concentrated, with one-pointed minds, detached from phenomena.

"Monks, those monks who are juniors, not long gone forth, recently come to this Dhamma and discipline, should be enjoined, settled, and established by you in the development of these four establishments of mindfulness."

4. *Makkaṭasutta*
The Monkey (SN 47:7; V 148–49)

"There are, monks, impassable uneven places in the Himalayas, the king of mountains, that are not fit for traveling either by monkeys or human beings. There are impassable uneven places in the Himalayas, the king of mountains, that are fit for traveling by monkeys but not by human beings. There are in the Himalayas, the king of mountains, even regions that are delightful, fit for traveling both by monkeys and human beings. There hunters set out glue on the monkey trails for trapping monkeys.

"When wise and cautious monkeys see that glue, they avoid it from afar. But a foolish and frivolous monkey approaches that glue and grabs it with his hand; he is bound there. Thinking, 'I will release my hand,' he grabs it with his second hand; he is bound there. Thinking, 'I will release both hands,' he grabs it with his foot; he is bound there. Thinking, 'I will release both hands and the foot,' he grabs it with his second foot; he is bound there. Thinking, 'I will release both hands and feet,' he grabs it with his snout; he is bound there.

"Thus that monkey, trapped in five places, lies there screeching. He has incurred misery, incurred disaster, to be done with by the hunter as he desires. Having speared him, the hunter raises the monkey on that [spear] itself, suspends [him from it],[79] and departs wherever he desires. This is what happens to one who wanders outside his own range into the domain of others.

"Therefore, monks, do not wander outside your range into the domain of others. For those wandering outside their range into the domain of others, Māra will gain an opening, Māra will gain a basis.

"And what, monks, is outside the range of a monk, the domain of others? It is the five objects of sensual pleasure. What five? Forms cognizable by the eye that are wished for, desired, agreeable, of a pleasing nature, connected with sensuality, enticing; sounds cognizable by the ear . . . odors cognizable by the nose . . . tastes cognizable by the tongue . . . tactile objects cognizable by the body that are wished for, desired, agreeable, of a pleasing nature, connected with sensuality, enticing. This is outside the range of a monk, the domain of others.

"Wander in your range, monks, in your own ancestral domain. For those wandering in their range, in their own ancestral domain, Māra will not gain an opening, Māra will not gain a basis.

"And what, monks, is the range of a monk, his own ancestral domain? It is the four establishments of mindfulness. What four? Here, a monk dwells contemplating the body in the body, ardent, clearly comprehending, mindful, having removed longing and dejection in regard to the world; contemplating feelings in feelings . . . contemplating the mind in the mind . . . contemplating phenomena in phenomena, ardent, clearly comprehending, mindful, having removed longing and dejection in regard to the world. This is the range of a monk, his own ancestral domain."

5. *Gilānasutta*
Ill (SN 47:9; V 152–54)

[1. The Buddha falls ill]
Thus have I heard. On one occasion the Blessed One was dwelling at Vesālī in Beḷuva village. There the Blessed One addressed the monks: "Come, monks, enter the rains around Vesālī, wherever you have friends, acquaintances, and intimates. I myself will enter the rains right here in Beḷuva village."[80]

"Yes, Bhante," those monks replied to the Blessed One, and they entered the rains around Vesālī, wherever they had friends, acquaintances, and intimates. But the Blessed One entered the rains right there in Beḷuva village.

Then, when the Blessed One had entered the rains, a terrible affliction arose in him, with severe pains bordering on death, but the Blessed One endured them, mindful and clearly comprehending, without being distressed.

Then this occurred to the Blessed One: "It is not proper for me that I should attain final nibbāna without having addressed my attendants and without having taken leave of the monastic Sangha. Surely I should suppress this affliction by means of energy, determine to maintain my vitality, and live on." Then the Blessed One, having suppressed that illness by means of energy, having determined to maintain his vitality, lived on.

[2. Ānanda's wish]
Then the Blessed One recovered from illness. Not long after he had recovered, he came out from his dwelling and sat down in the seat prepared for him in the shade of his dwelling. Then the Venerable Ānanda approached the Blessed One, paid homage to him, sat down to one side, and said this to the Blessed One:

"It's fortunate for me, Bhante, that the Blessed One is comfortable; it's fortunate that the Blessed One is bearing up; it's fortunate that the Blessed One is healthy. However, Bhante, because of the Blessed One's illness my body had been as if drugged, the directions did not appear clearly to me, and even the teachings did not occur to me. However, I had at least this consolation: 'The Blessed One will not attain final nibbāna so long as he has not pronounced something concerning the monastic Sangha.'"

[3. The Buddha's rejoinder]
"What now, Ānanda, does the monastic Sangha expect of me? I have taught the Dhamma without making distinctions of an inside and an outside. The Tathāgata does not have a teacher's closed fist in regard to the teachings.[81]

"Surely, Ānanda, one who thinks: 'I will lead the monastic Sangha,' or 'The monastic Sangha is dependent on me'—he surely might pronounce something concerning the monastic Sangha. But, Ānanda, the Tathāgata does not think: 'I will lead the monastic Sangha,' or 'The monastic Sangha is dependent on me.' Why then, Ānanda, should the Tathāgata pronounce something concerning the monastic Sangha?

"Now, Ānanda, I am old, aged, elderly, at the end of my journey, at the end of life. I am eighty years of age. Just as, Ānanda, a dilapidated cart keeps going by means of an assortment of straps, just so the Tathāgata's body keeps going, as it were, by an assortment of straps.

"On whatever occasion, Ānanda, the Tathāgata, through non-attention to all marks, through the cessation of some feelings, enters and dwells in the markless concentration of mind,[82] on that occasion the Tathāgata's body is more comfortable.

[4. The Buddha's instruction]
"Therefore, Ānanda, dwell with yourselves as an island, with yourselves as a refuge, with no other refuge, with the Dhamma as an island, with the Dhamma as a refuge, with no other refuge.[83] And how, Ānanda, does a monk dwell with himself as an island, with himself as a refuge, with no other refuge, with the Dhamma as an island, with the Dhamma as a refuge, with no other refuge?

"Here, Ānanda, a monk dwells contemplating the body in the body, ardent, clearly comprehending, mindful, having removed longing and dejection in regard to the world; he dwells contemplating feelings in feelings . . . contemplating the mind in the mind . . . contemplating phenomena in phenomena, ardent, clearly comprehending, mindful, having removed longing and dejection in regard to the world. It is in such a way, Ānanda, that a monk dwells with himself as an island, with himself as a refuge, with no other refuge, with the Dhamma as an island, with the Dhamma as a refuge, with no other refuge.

"Those who, either now or after my passing, will dwell with themselves as an island, with themselves as a refuge, with no other refuge, with the Dhamma as an island, with the Dhamma as a refuge, with no other refuge—for me, Ānanda, these monks will be topmost of those who desire the training."

6. *Sedakasutta*
Sedaka (SN 47:19; V 168–69)

On one occasion the Blessed One was dwelling among the Sumbhas where there was a town of the Sumbhas named Sedaka. There the Blessed One addressed the monks: "In the past, monks, an acrobat set up his bamboo pole and addressed his apprentice Medakathālikā: 'Come, dear Medakathālikā, climb up the bamboo pole and stand upon my shoulders.' Having replied to the acrobat, 'Yes, teacher,' the apprentice Medakathālikā climbed up the bamboo pole and stood upon the teacher's shoulders.

"Then the acrobat said this to the apprentice Medakathālikā: 'Dear Medakathālikā, you protect me, and I will protect you. Thus guarded by one another, protected by one another, we will display our skills, gain a profit, and safely descend from the bamboo pole.'

"When such was said, the apprentice Medakathālikā said this to the acrobat: 'That, teacher, isn't the way to do it. You, teacher, protect yourself, and I will protect myself. Thus self-guarded and self-protected, we will display our skills, gain a profit, and safely descend from the bamboo pole.'

"That is the method there," the Blessed One said, "as the apprentice Medakathālikā said to the teacher. 'I will protect myself,' monks, thus the establishment of mindfulness should be practiced; 'I will protect others,' thus the establishment of mindfulness should be practiced. Protecting oneself, one protects others; protecting others, one protects oneself.

"And how, monks, by protecting oneself does one protect others? By regular practice, by development, by cultivation [of the four establishments of mindfulness]: thus by protecting oneself, one protects others. And how, monks, by protecting others does one protect oneself? By patience, by harmlessness, by a mind of loving-kindness, by sympathy: thus by protecting others, one protects oneself.

"'I will protect myself,' monks, thus the establishment of mindfulness should be practiced. 'I will protect others,' thus the establishment of mindfulness should be practiced. Protecting oneself, one protects others; protecting others, one protects oneself."

7. *Janapadakalyāṇīsutta*
The Country Belle (SN 47:20; V 169–70)

"Suppose, monks, having heard 'the country belle, the country belle,' a great crowd of people would assemble. That country belle would be a supreme performer in dancing, a supreme performer in singing. Having heard 'the country belle is dancing and singing,' an even greater crowd of people would assemble.

"Then a man would come along who desires to live and does not desire to die, who desires happiness and is averse to suffering. They would say to him: 'You must carry around this bowl of oil, filled to the brim, between the great assembly and the country belle. A man with uplifted sword will follow right behind you. Wherever you spill even a little of this, just there he will fell your head.'

"What do you think about this, monks? Would that man stop paying attention to that bowl of oil and, due to heedlessness, direct his attention outwardly?"—"Certainly not, Bhante."

"This simile, monks, has been made by me for the purpose of communicating a meaning. And this is the meaning here: 'The bowl of oil filled to the brim'—this is a designation for mindfulness directed to the body. Therefore, monks, you should train thus: 'Mindfulness directed to the body will be developed and cultivated by us, made a vehicle, made a basis, stabilized, repeated, and well undertaken.' Thus indeed, monks, you should train."

8. *Sirivaḍḍhasutta*
Sirivaḍḍha (SN 47:29; V 176–77)

On one occasion the Venerable Ānanda was dwelling at Rājagaha in the bamboo grove, in the squirrels' feeding ground. Now on that occasion the householder Sirivaḍḍha was afflicted, sick, severely ill.

Then the householder Sirivaḍḍha addressed a man: "Come, man, approach the Venerable Ānanda. On my behalf venerate the Venerable Ānanda's feet with your head and say: 'The householder Sirivaḍḍha, Bhante, is afflicted, sick, severely ill. He venerates the Venerable Ānanda's feet with his head.' And then say thus: 'Please, Bhante, let the Venerable Ānanda come to the householder Sirivaḍḍha's residence out of compassion.'"

"Yes, sir," that man replied. Then he approached the Venerable Ānanda, paid homage to him, sat down to one side, and said this: "Bhante, the householder Sirivaḍḍha is afflicted, sick, severely ill. He venerates the Venerable Ānanda's feet with his head and says: 'Please, Bhante, let the Venerable Ānanda come to the householder Sirivaḍḍha's residence out of compassion.'" The Venerable Ānanda consented by silence.

Then in the morning the Venerable Ānanda dressed, took his bowl and outer robe, and went to the householder Sirivaḍḍha's residence. There he sat down in the prepared seat and said this to the householder Sirivaḍḍha: "Are you bearing up, householder? Is your health improving? Are your painful feelings retreating, not advancing, so that their retreat, not their advance, is discerned?"

"I am not bearing up, Bhante, my health is not improving. My severe painful feelings are advancing, not retreating, so that their advance, not their retreat, is discerned."

"Therefore, householder, you should train thus: 'I will dwell contemplating the body in the body, ardent, clearly comprehending, mindful, having removed longing and dejection in regard to the world; I will dwell contemplating feelings in feelings . . . contemplating the mind in the mind . . . contemplating phenomena in phenomena, ardent, clearly comprehending, mindful, having removed longing and dejection in regard to the world.' It is in such a way, householder, that you should train."

"Bhante, as to these four establishments of mindfulness that have been taught by the Blessed One, those things are found in me and I am seen engaging in those things. For, Bhante, I dwell contemplating the body in the body, ardent, clearly comprehending, mindful, having removed longing and dejection in regard to the world; I dwell contemplating feelings in feelings . . . contemplating the mind in the mind . . . contemplating phenomena in phenomena, ardent, clearly comprehending, mindful, having removed longing and dejection in regard to the world.

"And, Bhante, as to those five lower fetters taught by the Blessed One, I do not perceive in myself any of them that has not been abandoned."

"That is a gain for you, householder, that is well gained by you, householder! You have declared the fruit of a non-returner."[84]

2. The Seven Factors of Enlightenment

1. *Himavantasutta*
The Himalayas (SN 46:1; V 63–64)

"Monks, based on the Himalayas, the king of mountains, nāgas grow their bodies and acquire strength.[85] Having grown their bodies and acquired strength there, they enter the little pools, then the large pools, then the little rivers, then the large rivers. Having entered the large rivers, they enter the great ocean.

There they achieve greatness and vastness with respect to the body.

"Just so, monks, based on good behavior, established in good behavior, developing the seven factors of enlightenment, cultivating the seven factors of enlightenment, a monk acquires greatness and vastness in [wholesome] qualities.

"And how does a monk, based on good behavior, established in good behavior, developing the seven factors of enlightenment, cultivating the seven factors of enlightenment, acquire greatness and vastness in [wholesome] qualities? Here, a monk develops the enlightenment factor of mindfulness, which is based on seclusion, based on dispassion, based on cessation, evolving toward relinquishment.[86] He develops the enlightenment factor of discrimination of qualities . . . the enlightenment factor of energy . . . the enlightenment factor of rapture . . . the enlightenment factor of tranquility . . . the enlightenment factor of concentration . . . the enlightenment factor of equanimity, which is based on seclusion, based on dispassion, based on cessation, evolving toward relinquishment.

"It is in such a way that a monk, based on good behavior, established in good behavior, developing the seven factors of enlightenment, cultivating the seven factors of enlightenment, acquires greatness and vastness in [wholesome] qualities."

2. *Kāyasutta*
Body (SN 46:2; V 64–67)

[1. The nutriments for the hindrances]
"Just as, monks, this body is subsistent on nutriment, subsists in dependence on nutriment, and does not subsist without nutriment, just so the five hindrances are subsistent on nutriment, subsist in dependence on nutriment, and do not subsist without nutriment.

"And what, monks, is the nutriment for the arising of unarisen sensual desire and for the increase and expansion of arisen sensual desire? There is a beautiful object. The cultivation of superficial attention to this is the nutriment for the arising of unarisen sensual desire and for the increase and expansion of arisen sensual desire.

"And what, monks, is the nutriment for the arising of unarisen ill will and for the increase and expansion of arisen ill will? There is an object of aversion. The cultivation of superficial attention to this is the nutriment for the arising of unarisen ill will and for the increase and expansion of arisen ill will.

"And what, monks, is the nutriment for the arising of unarisen dullness and drowsiness and for the increase and expansion of arisen dullness and drowsiness? There is discontent, lethargy, yawning, tiredness after meals, and sluggishness of mind. The cultivation of superficial attention to these is the nutriment for the arising of unarisen dullness and drowsiness and for the increase and expansion of arisen dullness and drowsiness.

"And what, monks, is the nutriment for the arising of unarisen restlessness and regret and for the increase and expansion of arisen restlessness and regret? There is disquietude of mind. The cultivation of superficial attention to this is the nutriment for the arising of unarisen restlessness and regret and for the increase and expansion of arisen restlessness and regret.

"And what, monks, is the nutriment for the arising of unarisen doubt and for the increase and expansion of arisen doubt? There are things that are the basis for doubt. The cultivation of superficial attention to this is the nutriment for the arising of unarisen doubt and for the increase and expansion of arisen doubt.

"Just as, monks, this body is subsistent on nutriment, subsists in dependence on nutriment, and does not subsist without nutriment, just so these five hindrances are subsistent on nutriment, subsist in dependence on nutriment, and do not subsist without nutriment.

[2. The nutriments for the factors of enlightenment]

"Just as, monks, this body is subsistent on nutriment, subsists in dependence on nutriment, and does not subsist without nutriment, just so the seven factors of enlightenment are subsistent on nutriment, subsist in dependence on nutriment, and do not subsist without nutriment.

"And what, monks, is the nutriment for the arising of the unarisen enlightenment factor of mindfulness and for the fulfillment by development of the arisen enlightenment factor of mindfulness? There are, monks, things that are the basis for the enlightenment factor of mindfulness. The cultivation of thorough attention to them is the nutriment for the arising of the unarisen enlightenment factor of mindfulness and for the fulfillment by development of the arisen enlightenment factor of mindfulness.

"And what, monks, is the nutriment for the arising of the unarisen enlightenment factor of discrimination of qualities and for the fulfillment by development of the arisen enlightenment factor of discrimination of qualities? There are wholesome and unwholesome qualities, blameworthy and blameless qualities, inferior and superior qualities, qualities dark and bright with their counterparts.[87] The cultivation of thorough attention to them is the nutriment for the arising of the unarisen enlightenment factor of discrimination of qualities and for the fulfillment by development of the arisen enlightenment factor of discrimination of qualities.

"And what, monks, is the nutriment for the arising of the unarisen enlightenment factor of energy and for the fulfillment by development of the arisen enlightenment factor of energy? There are, monks, the element of arousal, the element of endeavor, the element of exertion.[88] The cultivation of thorough attention to them is the nutriment for the arising of the unarisen enlightenment factor of energy and for the fulfillment by development of the arisen enlightenment factor of energy.

"And what, monks, is the nutriment for the arising of the unarisen enlightenment factor of rapture and for the fulfillment by development of the arisen enlightenment factor of rapture? There are things that are the basis for the enlightenment factor of rapture. The cultivation of thorough attention to them is the nutriment for the arising of the unarisen enlightenment factor of rapture and for the fulfillment by development of the arisen enlightenment factor of rapture.

"And what, monks, is the nutriment for the arising of the unarisen enlightenment factor of tranquility and for the fulfillment by development of the arisen enlightenment factor of tranquility? There are, monks, tranquility of body and tranquility of mind. The cultivation of thorough attention to them is the nutriment for the arising of the unarisen enlightenment factor of tranquility and for the fulfillment by development of the arisen enlightenment factor of tranquility.

"And what, monks, is the nutriment for the arising of the unarisen enlightenment factor of concentration and for the fulfillment by development of the arisen enlightenment factor of concentration? There is an object of serenity, an object of non-diffusion.[89] The cultivation of thorough attention to this is the nutriment for the arising of the unarisen enlightenment factor of concentration and for the fulfillment by development of the arisen enlightenment factor of concentration.

"And what, monks, is the nutriment for the arising of the unarisen enlightenment factor of equanimity and for the fulfillment by development of the arisen enlightenment factor of equanimity? There are things that are the basis for the enlightenment factor of equanimity. The cultivation of thorough attention to them is the nutriment for the arising of the unarisen enlightenment factor of equanimity and for the fulfillment by development of the arisen enlightenment factor of equanimity.

"Just as, monks, this body is subsistent on nutriment, subsists in dependence on nutriment, and does not subsist without nutriment, just so these seven factors of enlightenment are subsistent on nutriment, subsist in dependence on nutriment, and do not subsist without nutriment."

3. *Sīlasutta*
Good Behavior (SN 46:3; V 67–70)

[1. Right association]
"Monks, as to those monks who are accomplished in good behavior, accomplished in concentration, accomplished in wisdom, accomplished in liberation, accomplished in the knowledge and vision of liberation: I say that the sight of those monks is helpful; I say that listening to those monks, too, is helpful; I say that approaching those monks, too, is helpful; I say that attending on those monks, too, is helpful; I say that recollecting those monks, too, is helpful; I say that following those monks in going forth, too, is helpful.

"For what reason? Because, having heard the Dhamma of such monks, one dwells withdrawn in two ways: by withdrawal of body and by withdrawal of mind. Dwelling thus withdrawn, one recollects and thinks over that Dhamma.

[2. The factors of enlightenment]
"When, monks, a monk dwelling thus withdrawn recollects and reflects on that Dhamma, on that occasion the enlightenment factor of mindfulness is aroused by the monk; on that occasion the monk develops the enlightenment factor of mindfulness; on that occasion the enlightenment factor of mindfulness goes to fulfillment by development for the monk.[90]

"Dwelling thus mindful, he discriminates that Dhamma with wisdom, examines it, and embarks upon an investigation into it. When a monk, dwelling thus mindful, discriminates that Dhamma with wisdom, examines it, and embarks upon an investigation into it, on that occasion the enlightenment factor of discrimination of qualities is aroused by the monk; on that occasion the monk develops the enlightenment factor of discrimination of qualities; on that occasion the enlightenment factor of discrimination of qualities goes to fulfillment by development for the monk.

"As he is discriminating that Dhamma with wisdom, examining it, and embarking upon an investigation into it, unsluggish energy is aroused. When unsluggish energy is aroused in a monk as he is discriminating that Dhamma with wisdom, examining it, and embarking upon an investigation into it, on that occasion the enlightenment factor of energy is aroused by the monk; on that occasion the monk develops the enlightenment factor of energy; on that occasion the enlightenment factor of energy goes to fulfillment by development for the monk.

"For one with energy aroused there arises non-carnal rapture. When, for a monk with energy aroused, there arises non-carnal rapture, on that occasion the enlightenment factor of rapture is aroused by the monk; on that occasion the monk develops the enlightenment factor of rapture; on that occasion the enlightenment factor of rapture goes to fulfillment by development for the monk.

"For one with a mind of rapture, the body becomes tranquil and the mind becomes tranquil. When, for a monk with a mind of rapture, the body becomes tranquil and the mind becomes tranquil, on that occasion the enlightenment factor of tranquility is aroused by the monk; on that occasion the monk develops the enlightenment factor of tranquility; on that occasion the enlightenment factor of tranquility goes to fulfillment by development for the monk.

"For one tranquil in body, who is happy, the mind becomes concentrated. When, for a monk tranquil in body, who is happy, the mind becomes concentrated, on that occasion the enlightenment factor of concentration is aroused by the monk; on that occasion the monk develops the enlightenment factor of concentration; on that occasion the enlightenment factor of concentration goes to fulfillment by development for the monk.

"He is one who observes well with equanimity the mind thus concentrated. When a monk is one who observes well with equanimity the mind thus concentrated, on that occasion the enlightenment factor of equanimity is aroused by the monk; on that occasion the monk develops the enlightenment factor of equanimity; on that occasion the enlightenment factor of equanimity goes to fulfillment by development for the monk.

[3. Seven fruits and benefits]

"Monks, when these seven factors of enlightenment have been developed and cultivated in this way, seven fruits and benefits may be expected. What are the seven fruits and benefits?

"One attains final knowledge early in this very life.[91]

"If one does not attain final knowledge early in this very life, then one attains final knowledge at the time of death.

"If one does not attain final knowledge early in this very life or at the time of death, then with the utter destruction of the five lower fetters one becomes an attainer of nibbāna in the interval.[92]

"If one does not attain final knowledge early in this very life . . . or become an attainer of nibbāna in the interval, then with the utter destruction of the five lower fetters one becomes an attainer of nibbāna upon landing.

"If one does not attain final knowledge early in this very life . . . or become an attainer of nibbāna upon landing, then with the utter destruction of the five lower fetters one becomes an attainer of nibbāna without exertion.

"If one does not attain final knowledge early in this very life . . . or become an attainer of nibbāna without exertion, then with the utter destruction of the five lower fetters one becomes an attainer of nibbāna with exertion.

"If one does not attain final knowledge early in this very life . . . or become an attainer of nibbāna with exertion, then with the utter destruction of the five lower fetters one is bound upstream, heading toward the Akaniṭṭha realm.[93]

"When, monks, the seven factors of enlightenment have been developed and cultivated in this way, these seven fruits and benefits may be expected."

4. *Bhikkhusutta*
A Monk (SN 46:5; V 72)

Then a certain monk approached the Blessed One . . . and said this: "They are called, Bhante, 'factors of enlightenment, factors of enlightenment.' In what way, Bhante, are they called 'factors of enlightenment'?"

"They lead to enlightenment, monk, therefore they are called 'factors of enlightenment.' Here, a monk develops the enlightenment factor of mindfulness, which is based on seclusion, based on dispassion, based on cessation, evolving toward relinquishment. . . . He develops the enlightenment factor of equanimity, which is based on seclusion, based on dispassion, based on cessation, evolving toward relinquishment.

"For one developing these seven factors of enlightenment, the mind is liberated from the influx of sensuality, from the influx of existence, from the influx of ignorance. In regard to what is liberated, the knowledge occurs thus: 'Liberated.' He understands: 'Finished is birth, the spiritual life has been lived, what had to be done has been done, there is no further for this state of being.' They lead to enlightenment, monk, therefore they are called 'factors of enlightenment.'"

5. *Kuṇḍaliyasutta*
Kuṇḍaliya (SN 46:6; V 73–75)

[1. The wanderer's questions]
On one occasion the Blessed One was dwelling at Sāketa in the Añjana Grove in the deer park. Then the wanderer Kuṇḍaliya approached the Blessed One and exchanged greetings with him. When they had concluded their greetings and cordial talk, he sat down to one side and said this to the Blessed One:

"Master Gotama, I am one who sits down in parks and frequents assemblies. After my breakfast, it is my custom to walk and wander from park to park, from garden to garden. There I see some ascetics and brahmins engaging in talk for the benefit of freeing [their doctrines from criticism] in debate and for the benefit of refuting [the doctrines of others]. But for what benefit does Master Gotama live?"

"The Tathāgata, Kuṇḍaliya, lives for the fruit and benefit of clear knowledge and liberation."

"But, Master Gotama, what things, developed and cultivated, fulfill clear knowledge and liberation?"

"The seven factors of enlightenment, Kuṇḍaliya, when developed and cultivated, fulfill clear knowledge and liberation."

"But, Master Gotama, what things, when developed and cultivated, fulfill the seven factors of enlightenment?"

"The four establishments of mindfulness, Kuṇḍaliya, when developed and cultivated, fulfill the seven factors of enlightenment."

"But, Master Gotama, what things, when developed and cultivated, fulfill the four establishments of mindfulness?"

"The three kinds of good conduct, Kuṇḍaliya, when developed and cultivated, fulfill the four establishments of mindfulness."

"But, Master Gotama, what things, when developed and cultivated, fulfill the three kinds of good conduct?"

"Restraint of the sense faculties, Kuṇḍaliya, when developed and cultivated, fulfills the three kinds of good conduct."

[2. Restraint of the senses]

"And how, Kuṇḍaliya, is restraint of the sense faculties developed and cultivated so that it fulfills the three kinds of good conduct? Here, having seen a form with the eye, a monk does not long for one that is agreeable, does not rejoice in it, does not lust for it. His body is steady and his mind is steady, inwardly well composed, well liberated.

"But having seen a form with the eye, he is not dismayed by one that is disagreeable, not daunted in mind, not dejected in mind, without ill will. His body is steady and his mind is steady, inwardly well composed and well liberated.

"Further, having heard a sound with the ear . . . having

smelled an odor with the nose . . . having tasted a taste with the tongue . . . having felt a tactile object with the body . . . having cognized a mental object with the mind, a monk does not long for one that is agreeable, does not rejoice in it, does not lust for it. His body is steady and his mind is steady, inwardly well composed and well liberated. But having cognized a mental object with the mind, he is not dismayed by one that is disagreeable, not daunted in mind, not dejected in mind, without ill will. His body is steady and his mind is steady, inwardly well composed and well liberated.

"When, Kuṇḍaliya, after he has seen a form with the eye, a monk's body is steady and his mind is steady, inwardly well composed and well liberated in regard to agreeable and disagreeable forms; when, after he has heard a sound with the ear . . . smelled an odor with the nose . . . tasted a taste with the tongue . . . felt a tactile object with the body . . . cognized a mental object with the mind, a monk's body is steady and his mind is steady, inwardly well composed and well liberated in regard to agreeable and disagreeable mental objects, then his restraint of the sense faculties has been developed and cultivated in such a way that it fulfills the three kinds of good conduct.

[3. From good conduct to liberation]

"And how, Kuṇḍaliya, are the three kinds of good conduct developed and cultivated so that they fulfill the four establishments of mindfulness? Here, having abandoned misconduct of body, a monk develops good conduct of body; having abandoned misconduct of speech, he develops good conduct of speech; having abandoned misconduct of mind, he develops good conduct of mind. When the three kinds of good conduct have been developed and cultivated in such a way, they fulfill the four establishments of mindfulness.

"And how, Kuṇḍaliya, are the four establishments of mindfulness developed and cultivated so that they fulfill the seven factors of enlightenment? Here, a monk dwells contemplating the body in the body, ardent, clearly comprehending, mindful, having removed longing and dejection in regard to the world; he dwells contemplating feelings in feelings . . . contemplating the mind in the mind . . . contemplating phenomena in phenomena, ardent, clearly comprehending, mindful, having removed longing and dejection in regard to the world. When the four establishments of mindfulness have been developed and cultivated in such a way, they fulfill the seven factors of enlightenment.

"And how, Kuṇḍaliya, are the seven factors of enlightenment developed and cultivated so that they fulfill clear knowledge and liberation? Here, a monk develops the enlightenment factor of mindfulness, which is based on seclusion, based on dispassion, based on cessation, evolving toward relinquishment. . . . He develops the enlightenment factor of equanimity, which is based on seclusion, based on dispassion, based on cessation, evolving toward relinquishment. When the seven factors of enlightenment have been developed and cultivated in such a way, they fulfill clear knowledge and liberation."

[4. Going for refuge]
When such was said, the wanderer Kuṇḍaliya said this to the Blessed One: "Excellent, Master Gotama, excellent, Master Gotama! Just as one would turn upright what had been overturned, or would reveal what was concealed, or would point out the path to one who is lost, or would hold up an oil lamp in the darkness, thinking, 'Those with eyes will see forms,' just so the Dhamma has been revealed in many ways by Master Gotama.

"I go to Master Gotama for refuge, to the Dhamma, and to the monastic Sangha. Let Master Gotama consider me a lay disciple who from today has gone for refuge for as long as life lasts."

6. *Gilānasutta*
Ill (SN 46:14; V 79–80)

On one occasion the Blessed One was dwelling at Rājagaha in the bamboo grove, in the squirrels' feeding ground. Now on that occasion the Venerable Mahākassapa was dwelling in the Pipphali Cave, afflicted, sick, severely ill. Then in the evening, when he emerged from seclusion, the Blessed One approached the Venerable Mahākassapa, sat down in the prepared seat, and said this to the Venerable Mahākassapa: "Are you bearing up, Kassapa? Is your health improving? Are your painful feelings retreating, not advancing, so that their retreat, not their advance, is discerned?"

"I am not bearing up, Bhante, my health is not improving. My severe painful feelings are advancing, not retreating, so that their advance, not their retreat, is discerned."

"These seven factors of enlightenment, Kassapa, rightly expounded by me, when developed and cultivated, lead to direct knowledge, to enlightenment, to nibbāna. What seven? The enlightenment factor of mindfulness, Kassapa, rightly expounded by me, when developed and cultivated, leads to direct knowledge, to enlightenment, to nibbāna. . . . The enlightenment factor of equanimity, rightly expounded by me, when developed and cultivated, leads to direct knowledge, to enlightenment, to nibbāna. These seven factors of enlightenment, Kassapa, rightly expounded by me, when developed and cultivated, lead to direct knowledge, to enlightenment, to nibbāna."

"Certainly, Blessed One, they are enlightenment factors! Certainly, Fortunate One, they are enlightenment factors!"

This is what the Blessed One said. Elated, the Venerable Mahākassapa delighted in the Blessed One's statement. And the Venerable Mahākassapa recovered from that illness. And thus that illness was abandoned by the Venerable Mahākassapa.

7. *Aggisutta*
Fire (SN 46:53; V 112–15)

[1. The challenge]
Then, in the morning, a number of monks dressed and, taking their bowls and outer robes, entered Sāvatthī for alms. Then it occurred to them: "It is still too early to walk for alms in Sāvatthī. Let us go to the park of the wanderers of other sects."

Then those monks went to the park of the wanderers of other sects. They exchanged greetings with those wanderers and, when they had concluded their greetings and cordial talk, sat down to one side. The wanderers then said to them: "Friends, the ascetic Gotama teaches the Dhamma to his disciples thus: 'Come, monks, abandon the five hindrances, the corruptions of the mind that weaken wisdom, and develop correctly the seven factors of enlightenment.' We too teach the Dhamma to our disciples thus: 'Come, friends, abandon the five hindrances, the corruptions of the mind that weaken wisdom, and develop correctly the seven factors of enlightenment.' So, friends, what here is the distinction, the disparity, the difference between the ascetic Gotama and us—that is, regarding the one Dhamma teaching and the other, the one manner of instruction and the other?"

Then those monks neither delighted in nor rejected the statement of those wanderers. Without delighting in it, without rejecting it, they rose from their seats and left, thinking, "We shall learn the meaning of this statement in the presence of the Blessed One."

Then, when those monks had walked for alms in Sāvatthī and had returned from the alms round, after their meal they approached the Blessed One, paid homage to him, and sat down to one side. They then reported their entire discussion with those wanderers. [The Blessed One said this:]

"Wanderers of other sects who speak thus should be told: 'On an occasion, friends, when the mind is sluggish, on that occasion which factors of enlightenment is it not the time to develop, and which factors of enlightenment is it the time to develop? But on an occasion when the mind is excited, on that occasion which factors of enlightenment is it not the time to develop, and which factors of enlightenment is it the time to develop?'

"Asked thus, monks, wanderers of other sects will not succeed in replying, and further, they will incur distress. For what reason? Because, monks, that is not in their domain.

"I do not see anyone in the world with its devas, with Māra, with Brahmā, in this population with its ascetics and brahmins, with its devas and humans, who could satisfy the mind with an answer to these questions apart from the Tathāgata or a disciple of the Tathāgata or one who has heard it from here.

[2. Stimulating the sluggish mind]

"On an occasion, monks, when the mind is sluggish, on that occasion it is not the time to develop the enlightenment factor of tranquility, the enlightenment factor of concentration, and the enlightenment factor of equanimity. For what reason? Because the mind is sluggish; it is hard to arouse it with these things.

"Suppose, monks, a person would desire to cause a small fire to blaze up. He would throw wet grass, wet cow dung, and wet sticks upon it, and would spray water over it, and would sprinkle it with soil. Would that person be capable of causing a small fire to blaze up?"—"Certainly not, Bhante."

"Just so, monks, on an occasion when the mind is sluggish, on that occasion it is not the time to develop the enlightenment factor of tranquility, the enlightenment factor of concentration, and the enlightenment factor of equanimity. For what reason? Because the mind is sluggish; it is hard to arouse it with these things.

"On an occasion, monks, when the mind is sluggish, on that occasion it is the time to develop the enlightenment factor of discrimination of qualities, the enlightenment factor of energy, and the enlightenment factor of rapture. For what reason? Because the mind is sluggish; it is easy to arouse it with these things.

"Suppose, monks, a person would desire to cause a small fire to blaze up. He would throw dry grass, dry cow dung, and dry sticks upon it, and would blow on it with his mouth, and would not sprinkle it with soil. Would that person be capable of causing a small fire to blaze up?"—"Yes, Bhante."

"Just so, monks, on an occasion when the mind is sluggish, on that occasion it is the time to develop the enlightenment factor of discrimination of qualities, the enlightenment factor of energy, and the enlightenment factor of rapture. For what reason? Because the mind is sluggish; it is easy to arouse it with these things.

[3. Calming the excited mind]

"On an occasion, monks, when the mind is excited, on that occasion it is not the time to develop the enlightenment factor of discrimination of qualities, the enlightenment factor of energy, and the enlightenment factor of rapture. For what reason? Because the mind is excited; it is hard to calm it down with these things.

"Suppose, monks, a person would desire to extinguish a large bonfire. He would throw dry grass, dry cow dung, and dry sticks upon it, and would blow on it with his mouth, and would not sprinkle it with soil. Would that person be capable of extinguishing a large bonfire?"—"Certainly not, Bhante."

"Just so, monks, on an occasion when the mind is excited, on that occasion it is not the time to develop the enlightenment factor of discrimination of qualities, the enlightenment factor of energy, and the enlightenment factor of rapture. For what reason? Because the mind is excited; it is hard to calm it down with these things.

"On an occasion, monks, when the mind is excited, on that occasion it is the time to develop the enlightenment factor of tranquility, the enlightenment factor of concentration, and the enlightenment factor of equanimity. For what reason? Because the mind is excited; it is easy to calm it down with these things.

"Suppose, monks, a person would desire to extinguish a large bonfire. He would throw wet grass, wet cow dung, and wet sticks upon it, and would spray it with water, and would sprinkle it with soil. Would that person be capable of extinguishing a large bonfire?"—"Yes, Bhante."

"Just so, monks, on an occasion when the mind is excited, on that occasion it is the time to develop the enlightenment factor of tranquility, the enlightenment factor of concentration, and the enlightenment factor of equanimity. For what reason? Because the mind is excited; it is easy to calm it down with these things.

"But mindfulness, monks, I say is useful everywhere."

3. The Noble Eightfold Path

1. *Upaḍḍhasutta*
Half (SN 45:2; V 2–3)

On one occasion the Blessed One was dwelling among the Sakyans, where there was a town of the Sakyans named Nāgaraka. Then the Venerable Ānanda approached the Blessed One, paid homage to him, sat down to one side, and said this to the Blessed One: "This is half of the spiritual life, Bhante—that is, good friendship, good companionship, good comradeship."[94]

"Do not speak thus, Ānanda! Do not speak thus, Ānanda! This is indeed the whole spiritual life, Ānanda—that is, good friendship, good companionship, good comradeship. Of a monk who has a good friend, a good companion, a good comrade,[95] it is to be expected that he will develop and cultivate the noble eightfold path.

"And how, Ānanda, does a monk who has a good friend, a good companion, a good comrade, develop and cultivate the noble eightfold path? Here, a monk develops right view, which is based on seclusion, based on dispassion, based on cessation, evolving toward relinquishment; he develops right intention . . . right speech . . . right action . . . right livelihood . . . right effort . . . right mindfulness . . . right concentration, which is based on seclusion, based on dispassion, based on cessation, evolving toward relinquishment. It is in such a way, Ānanda, that a monk who has a good friend, a good companion, a good comrade develops and cultivates the noble eightfold path.

"In this way, too, Ānanda, can it be understood how this is indeed the whole spiritual life—that is, good friendship, good companionship, good comradeship. By relying on me as a good friend, Ānanda, beings subject to birth are freed from birth; beings subject to old age are freed from old age; beings subject to death are freed from death; beings subject to sorrow, lamentation, pain, dejection, and misery are freed from sorrow, lamentation, pain, dejection, and misery. In this way, too, Ānanda, it can be understood how this is the whole spiritual life—that is, good friendship, good companionship, good comradeship."

2. *Kimatthiyasutta*
For What Purpose? (SN 45:5; V 6–7)

Then several monks approached the Blessed One. . . . and said this to the Blessed One: "Here, Bhante, wanderers belonging to other sects ask us thus: 'For what purpose, friends, is the spiritual life lived under the ascetic Gotama?' When we are asked thus, Bhante, we answer those wanderers thus: 'The spiritual life, friends, is lived under the Blessed One for the full understanding of suffering.'

"Is it the case, Bhante, that when we are asked thus and answer thus, we are stating what has been said by the Blessed One and do not falsely misrepresent him; that we answer in accordance with the Dhamma, and no reasonable consequence of our assertion is open to criticism?"

"Certainly, monks, when you are asked thus and answer thus, you state what has been said by me and do not falsely misrepresent me; you answer in accordance with the Dhamma, and no reasonable consequence of your assertion is open to criticism. Because it is for the full understanding of suffering that the spiritual life is lived under me.

"If, monks, wanderers belonging to other sects would ask you, 'But is there, friends, a path, is there a way, for the full understanding of this suffering?' being asked thus, you should answer those wanderers thus: 'There is, friends, a path, there is a way, for the full understanding of this suffering.'

"And what, monks, is the path, what is the way, for the full understanding of this suffering? It is just this noble eightfold path—that is, right view . . . right concentration. This, monks, is the path, this is the way, for the full understanding of this suffering. When you are asked thus, monks, you should thus answer those wanderers belonging to other sects."

3. *Vibhaṅgasutta*
Analysis (SN 45:8; V 8–10)

"I will teach you, monks, the noble eightfold path and I will analyze it. Listen to that and attend well. I will speak."—"Yes, Bhante," those monks replied. The Blessed One said this:

"And what, monks, is the noble eightfold path? It is this: right view, right intention, right speech, right action, right livelihood, right effort, right mindfulness, and right concentration.

"And what, monks, is right view? Knowledge of suffering, knowledge of the origin of suffering, knowledge of the cessation of suffering, knowledge of the way leading to the cessation of suffering: this is called right view.

"And what, monks, is right intention? The intention of renunciation, the intention of goodwill, the intention of harmlessness: this is called right intention.

"And what, monks, is right speech? Abstinence from false speech, abstinence from divisive speech, abstinence from harsh speech, abstinence from idle chatter: this is called right speech.

"And what, monks, is right action? Abstinence from the destruction of life, abstinence from taking what is not given, abstinence from sexual misconduct:[96] this is called right action.

"And what, monks, is right livelihood? Here, a noble disciple, having abandoned wrong livelihood, earns his living by right livelihood: this is called right livelihood.

"And what, monks, is right effort? Here, a monk generates desire for the non-arising of unarisen bad unwholesome qualities; he makes an effort, arouses energy, applies his mind, and strives. He generates desire for the abandoning of arisen evil unwholesome qualities. . . . He generates desire for the arising of unarisen wholesome qualities. . . . He generates desire for the continuation of arisen wholesome qualities, for their non-decline, increase, expansion, and fulfillment by development; he makes an effort, arouses energy, applies his mind, and strives. This is called right effort.

"And what, monks, is right mindfulness? Here, a monk dwells contemplating the body in the body, ardent, clearly comprehending, mindful, having removed longing and dejection in regard to the world; contemplating feelings in feelings, ardent, clearly comprehending, mindful, having removed longing and dejection in regard to the world; contemplating the mind in the mind, ardent, clearly comprehending, mindful, having removed longing and dejection in regard to the world; contemplating phenomena in phenomena, ardent, clearly comprehending, mindful, having removed longing and dejection in regard to the world. This is called right mindfulness.

"And what, monks, is right concentration? Here, secluded from sensual pleasures, secluded from unwholesome qualities, a monk enters and dwells in the first jhāna, which is accompanied by thought, accompanied by examination, with rapture and pleasure born of seclusion.

"Through the subsiding of thought and examination, he enters and dwells in the second jhāna, [marked by] internal placidity and unification of mind, which is without thought, without examination, with rapture and pleasure born of concentration.

"And with the fading away of rapture, he dwells equanimous, mindful and clearly comprehending, and he experiences pleasure with the body; he enters and dwells in the third jhāna on account of which the noble ones declare of him: 'He is equanimous, mindful, dwelling pleasantly.'

"Through the abandoning of pleasure and the abandoning of pain, and through the passing away previously of joy and dejection, he enters and dwells in the fourth jhāna, which is neither painful nor pleasant and has the purification of mindfulness by equanimity. This is called right concentration."

4. *Paṭipadāsutta*
Practice (SN 45:24; V 18–19)

"Monks, I do not praise wrong practice, whether of a layperson or one gone forth. One practicing wrongly, whether a layperson or one gone forth, because of their undertaking of wrong practice, is not one who achieves the method, the Dhamma, the wholesome.

"And what, monks, is wrong practice? It is this: wrong view . . . wrong concentration. This is called wrong practice. I do not praise wrong practice, whether of a layperson or of one gone forth. One practicing wrongly, whether a layperson or one gone forth, because of their undertaking of wrong practice, is not one who achieves the method, the Dhamma, the wholesome.

"Monks, I praise right practice, whether of a layperson or of one gone forth. One practicing rightly, whether a layperson or one gone forth, because of their undertaking of right practice, is one who achieves the method, the Dhamma, the wholesome.

"And what, monks, is right practice? It is this: right view . . . right concentration. This is called right practice. I praise right practice, whether of a layperson or of one gone forth. One practicing rightly, whether a layperson or one gone forth, because of their undertaking of right practice, is one who achieves the method, the Dhamma, the wholesome."

5. *Kalyāṇamittasutta*
Good Friend (SN 45:49, 45:56; V 29–30, V 31)

"This, monks, is the forerunner, this is the sign for the rising of the sun—that is, the break of dawn. Just so, for a monk, this is the forerunner, this is the sign for the arising of the noble eightfold path—that is, good friendship. Of a monk who has a good friend, this is to be expected, that he will develop and cultivate the noble eightfold path.

(45:49) "And how, monks, does a monk who has a good friend develop and cultivate the noble eightfold path? Here, a monk develops right view . . . develops right concentration, which is based on seclusion, based on dispassion, based on cessation, evolving toward relinquishment. It is in such a way that a monk who has a good friend develops and cultivates the noble eightfold path.

(45:56) "And how, monks, does a monk who has a good friend develop and cultivate the noble eightfold path? Here, a monk develops right view . . . develops right concentration, which has as its culmination the removal of lust, the removal of hatred, the removal of delusion. It is in such a way that a monk who has a good friend develops and cultivates the noble eightfold path."

6. *Pācīnaninnasutta*
Slants to the East (SN 45:91, 45:103; V 38, V 40)

"Just as, monks, the Ganges River slants to the east, slopes to the east, inclines to the east, just so, a monk developing and cultivating the noble eightfold path slants to nibbāna, slopes to nibbāna, inclines to nibbāna.

(45:91) "And how, monks, does a monk developing and cultivating the noble eightfold path slant to nibbāna, slope to nibbāna, incline to nibbāna? Here, a monk develops right view . . . develops right concentration, which is based on seclusion, based on dispassion, based on cessation, evolving toward relinquishment. It is in such a way that a monk developing and cultivating the noble eightfold path slants to nibbāna, slopes to nibbāna, inclines to nibbāna.

(45:103) "And how, monks, does a monk developing and cultivating the noble eightfold path slant to nibbāna, slope to nibbāna, incline to nibbāna? Here, a monk develops right view . . . develops right concentration, which has as its culmination the removal of lust, the removal of hatred, the removal of delusion. It is in such a way that a monk developing and cultivating the noble eightfold path slants to nibbāna, slopes to nibbāna, inclines to nibbāna."

7. *Nadīsutta*
The River (SN 45:160; V 53–54)

"Monks, the Ganges River slants to the east, slopes to the east, inclines to the east. Suppose now a great crowd of people would come with a shovel and a basket, saying: 'We will make this Ganges River slant to the west, slope to the west, incline to the west.' What do you think, monks, can that great crowd of people make the Ganges River slant to the west, slope to the west, incline to the west?"

"Certainly not, Bhante. For what reason? The Ganges River slants to the east, slopes to the east, inclines to the east, so it is not easy to make it slant to the west, slope to the west, incline to the west. In the end that great crowd of people would only reap fatigue and distress."

"Just so, monks, kings or royal ministers, friends or associates, relatives or kinsfolk, might invite a monk who is developing and cultivating the noble eightfold path to receive wealth, saying: 'Come, good man, why should these dyed robes burn you? Why do you roam around with a shaved head and a begging bowl? Come, having reverted to the lay life, enjoy wealth and do meritorious deeds.'

"Monks, it is impossible that a monk who is developing and cultivating the noble eightfold path will reject the training and revert to the lay life. For what reason? Because for a long time his mind has slanted to seclusion, sloped to seclusion, inclined to seclusion, it is impossible that he will revert to the lay life.

"And how, monks, does a monk develop and cultivate the noble eightfold path? Here, a monk develops right view . . . develops right concentration, which is based on seclusion, based on dispassion, based on cessation, evolving toward relinquishment. It is in such a way that a monk develops the noble eightfold path, cultivates the noble eightfold path."

8. *Oghavagga*
The Chapter on the Floods (SN 45:171–180; V 58–62)

"Monks, there are these four floods. What four? The flood of sensuality, the flood of existence, the flood of views, the flood of ignorance. These are the four floods. This noble eightfold path is to be developed for direct knowledge of these four floods, for the full understanding of them, for their utter destruction, for their abandoning.

"Monks, there are these four bonds. What four? The bond of sensuality, the bond of existence, the bond of views, the bond of ignorance. These are the four bonds. This noble eightfold path is to be developed for direct knowledge of these four bonds, for the full understanding of them, for their utter destruction, for their abandoning.

"Monks, there are these four kinds of clinging. What four? Clinging to sensual pleasure, clinging to views, clinging to precepts and observances, clinging to a doctrine of self. These are the four kinds of clinging. This noble eightfold path is to be developed for direct knowledge of these four kinds of clinging, for the full understanding of them, for their utter destruction, for their abandoning.

"Monks, there are these four knots. What four? The bodily knot of covetousness, the bodily knot of ill will, the bodily knot of wrong grasp of precepts and observances, the bodily knot of adherence to dogmatic assertions of truth. These are the four knots. This noble eightfold path is to be developed for direct knowledge of these four knots, for the full understanding of them, for their utter destruction, for their abandoning.

"Monks, there are these seven tendencies. What seven? The tendency to sensual lust, the tendency to aversion, the tendency to views, the tendency to doubt, the tendency to conceit, the tendency to lust for existence, the tendency to ignorance. These are the seven tendencies. This noble eightfold path is to be developed for direct knowledge of these seven tendencies, for the full understanding of them, for their utter destruction, for their abandoning.

"Monks, there are these five cords of sensual pleasure. What five? Forms cognizable by the eye. . . . Sounds cognizable by the ear. . . . Odors cognizable by the nose. . . . Tastes cognizable by the tongue. . . . Tactile objects cognizable by the body that are wished for, desired, agreeable, of a pleasing nature, connected with sensuality, enticing. These are the five cords of sensual pleasure. This noble eightfold path is to be developed for direct knowledge of these five cords of sensual pleasure, for the full understanding of them, for their utter destruction, for their abandoning.

"Monks, there are these five hindrances. What five? The hindrance of sensual desire, the hindrance of ill will, the hindrance of dullness and drowsiness, the hindrance of restlessness and regret, the hindrance of doubt. These are the five hindrances. This noble eightfold path is to be developed for direct knowledge of these five hindrances, for the full understanding of them, for their utter destruction, for their abandoning.

"Monks, there are these five clinging-aggregates. What five? The form clinging-aggregate, the feeling clinging-aggregate, the perception clinging-aggregate, the volitional activities clinging-aggregate, the consciousness clinging-aggregate. These are the five clinging-aggregates. This noble eightfold path is to be developed for direct knowledge of these five clinging-aggregates, for the full understanding of them, for their utter destruction, for their abandoning.

"Monks, there are these five lower fetters. What five? The view of the personal-assemblage, doubt, wrong grasp of precepts and observances, sensual desire, and ill will. These are the five lower fetters. This noble eightfold path is to be developed for direct knowledge of these five lower fetters, for the full understanding of them, for their utter destruction, for their abandoning.

"Monks, there are these five higher fetters. What five? Lust for form, lust for the formless, conceit, restlessness, ignorance. These are the five higher fetters. This noble eightfold path is to be developed for direct knowledge of these five higher fetters, for the full understanding of them, for their utter destruction, for their abandoning.

"What noble eightfold path? Here, a monk develops right view . . . right concentration, which is based on seclusion, based on dispassion, based on cessation, evolving toward relinquishment. This noble eightfold path is to be developed for direct knowledge of these five higher fetters, for the full understanding of them, for their utter destruction, for their abandoning.

"What noble eightfold path? Here, monks, a monk develops right view . . . right concentration, which has as its culmination the removal of lust, the removal of hatred, the removal of delusion . . . which has the deathless as its ground, the deathless as its destination, the deathless as its culmination . . . which slants, slopes, and inclines toward nibbāna. This noble eightfold path is to be developed for direct knowledge of these five higher fetters, for the full understanding of them, for their utter destruction, for their abandoning."

6. The Unconditioned: The Goal

Introduction

The theme of this short chapter is the unconditioned (*asaṅkhata*), a designation for nibbāna. Whereas the cessation aspect of dependent origination included in chapter 4 shows the goal of the Dhamma through a series of negations, the present chapter shows the goal more directly and explicitly under thirty-two epithets, including nibbāna. As is characteristic of the Nikāyas, the goal is still described largely in negative terms: as the unconditioned, uninclined, unaging, undisintegrating, and so forth. Even the definition of the unconditioned as "the destruction of lust, the destruction of hatred, the destruction of delusion" has a negative ring.

When nibbāna is described as the destruction of lust, hatred, and delusion, this naturally gives rise to the question whether it is simply the eradication of defilements or a transcendent state or dimension that entails the destruction of the defilements. A sutta in the Itivuttaka (§44), a short canonical text, speaks of two "elements of nibbāna." The element of nibbāna with residue remaining (*sa-upādisesā nibbānadhātu*) is defined as the destruction of lust, hatred, and delusion achieved by the living arahant. But with respect to the element of nibbāna without residue remaining (*anupādisesā nibbānadhātu*), the text merely says that for the arahant, "all feelings, not being delighted in, will become cool right here." These two nibbāna elements respectively represent nibbāna during life and nibbāna attained with the passing away of the arahant, and in both cases their characterization here seems negative. But other suttas speak of nibbāna as a state that is "unborn, unproduced, unbecome, and unconditioned" (Udāna §73), or as a "base" (*āyatana*) where none of the conditioned phenomena of the world are to be found. In this base, it is said, there is "no coming, no going, no standing still; it is unestablished, unchanging, without arising and perishing, without a support" (Udāna §71). Such descriptions, while cryptic and still expressed by way of negations, point to nibbāna as a transcendent, ever-existent state that makes possible liberation from the round of birth and death.

Nibbāna itself is outside and beyond the five aggregates that constitute the existent person, but it is to be realized and experienced within the person by penetrating with wisdom the true nature of the five aggregates. The suttas never identify nibbāna with consciousness, which they always treat as a conditioned phenomenon, arisen in dependence on the sense bases and objects. But while unconditioned, nibbāna is to be known and seen by a constellation of mental factors occurring in a state of consciousness in which wisdom plays the dominant role. The consciousness that realizes nibbāna is a conditioned phenomenon, while nibbāna itself is unconditioned. This experiential realization of nibbāna is arrived at by cultivating the path that leads to the unconditioned, a path that brings together concentration and insight in harmonious balance. Thus a sutta tells us that when the monk has settled the mind and thoroughly contemplated the five aggregates as impermanent, suffering, and non-self, at a certain point "he turns the mind away from these things and focuses it on the deathless element" (*so tehi dhammehi cittaṃ paṭivāpetvā amatāya dhātuyā cittaṃ upasaṃharati*). Thereby he reaches either "the destruction of the influxes"—that is, arahantship—or the stage of non-returner (MN 64, I 435–36).

In the suttas that constitute the Asaṅkhatasaṃyutta, chapter 43 of the Saṃyutta Nikāya, the stress is not on a theoretical understanding of nibbāna but on the path that leads to the goal. The path is shown by taking first the term "unconditioned" (*asaṅkhata*) to represent the aim of practice and then highlighting the path from different angles. Though the path may be described differently in these suttas, the different descriptions merely foreground different groups of factors that enter into the path; they do not entail that there are different paths to the final goal.

The opening sutta proclaims mindfulness directed to the body to constitute the path. This sutta is then expanded upon in two steps. At the first step, it is elaborated upon by taking ten other sets of factors collectively as the way to the unconditioned. The ten are: (1) serenity and insight; (2) three kinds of concentration—that associated with thought and examination, that dissociated from thought but conjoined with examination, and that fully dissociated from both thought and examination; (3) three other kinds of concentration—the emptiness, signless, and wishless concentrations; (4) the four establishments of mindfulness; (5) the four right strivings; (6) the four bases for spiritual power; (7) the five spiritual faculties; (8) the five powers; (9) the seven factors of enlightenment; and (10) the noble eightfold path. Each set constitutes a separate sutta.

Hence, including mindfulness directed to the body, we obtain eleven suttas, SN 43:1–11. The next sutta, SN 43:12, contains forty-five subdivisions. Here, serenity and insight are each treated *separately* as the path to the unconditioned, and then each factor within the above-mentioned groups is treated as a distinct path to the unconditioned. Thus serenity and insight constitute two suttas, while the two sets of three concentrations give us six more. When we add these eight to the thirty-seven aids to enlightenment bundled into the seven groups, we obtain a total of forty-five suttas laying out the way to the unconditioned.

This entire pattern is then applied to the goal described by thirty-one other epithets, from the uninclined (*anata*) down to the destination (*parāyaṇa*). Since the path leading to the destination begins with mindfulness directed to the body, this means that fifty-six versions of the path (the eleven of 45:1–11 plus the forty-five of 45:12) are to be conjoined with each of the following thirty-one epithets of nibbāna for a total of 1,736 suttas. All printed editions of this chapter severely compress the presentation of the material, but it is possible that in the era when oral recitation prevailed, reciters would recite each sutta in full.

Each sutta obtained through this process of permutations ends with the same exhortation: "Meditate, monks, do not be heedless. Do not be regretful later. This is our instruction to you." Hence for the Buddha speculative theories about the final goal give way to the need for practical application. What prevails above all else is the effort to realize the goal in one's own experience.

1. *Asaṅkhatasutta*
The Unconditioned (SN 43:1; IV 359)

"I will teach you, monks, the unconditioned and the path leading to the unconditioned. Listen to that. And what, monks, is the unconditioned? The destruction of lust, the destruction of hatred, the destruction of delusion: this is called the unconditioned. And what is the path leading to the unconditioned? Mindfulness directed to the body: this is called the path leading to the unconditioned.

"Thus, monks, I have taught you the unconditioned, I have taught the path leading to the unconditioned. Whatever should be done by a teacher out of compassion for his disciples—by one desiring their welfare, by one who is compassionate—that I have done for you. These are the roots of trees, these are empty huts. Meditate, monks, do not be heedless. Do not be regretful later. This is our instruction to you."

2. *Anatasutta*, Etc.
The Uninclined, Etc. (SN 43:13–43; IV 368–73)

"I will teach you, monks, the uninclined and the path leading to the uninclined . . . I will teach you the influx-free . . . truth . . . the beyond . . . the subtle . . . the very hard to see . . . the unaging . . . the everlasting . . . the undisintegrating . . . the invisible . . . the unproliferated . . . the peaceful . . . the deathless . . . the sublime . . . the auspicious . . . the secure . . . the destruction of craving . . . the wondrous . . . the marvelous . . . the unailing . . . that not subject to ailing . . . nibbāna . . . the unafflicted . . . dispassion . . . freedom . . . non-attachment . . . the island . . . the cavern . . . the shelter . . . the refuge . . . the destination and the path leading to the destination. Listen to that. And what, monks, is the destination? The destruction of lust, the destruction of hatred, the destruction of delusion: this is called the destination. And what is the path leading to the destination? Mindfulness directed to the body: this is called the path leading to the destination.

"Thus, monks, I have taught you the destination, I have taught the path leading to the destination. Whatever should be done by a teacher out of compassion for his disciples—by one desiring their welfare, by one who is compassionate—that I have done for you. These are the roots of trees, these are empty huts. Meditate, monks, do not be heedless. Do not be regretful later. This is our instruction to you."

Pāli-English Glossary

1. *Cattāri ariyasaccāni*: the four noble truths
   dukkhaṃ ariyasaccaṃ: the noble truth of suffering
   dukkhasamudayaṃ ariyasaccaṃ: the noble truth of the origin of suffering
   dukkhanirodhaṃ ariyasaccaṃ: the noble truth of the cessation of suffering
   dukkhanirodhagāminī paṭipadā ariyasaccaṃ: the noble truth of the way leading to the cessation of suffering

2. *Pañcupādānakkhandhā*: the five clinging-aggregates
   rūpupādānakkhandha: the form clinging-aggregate
   vedanupādānakkhandha: the feeling clinging-aggregate
   saññupādānakkhandha: the perception clinging-aggregate
   saṅkhārupādānakkhandha: the volitional-activities clinging-aggregate
   viññāṇupādānakkhandha: the consciousness clinging-aggregate

3. *Cha ajjhattikāni āyatanānī*: the six internal sense bases
   cakkhāyatana: the eye-base
   sotāyatana: the ear-base
   ghānāyatana: the nose-base
   jivhāyatana: the tongue-base
   kāyāyatana: the body-base
   manāyatana: the mind-base

4. *Paṭiccasamuppada*: dependent origination
   avijjāpaccayā saṅkhārā: with ignorance as condition, volitional activities

saṅkhārapaccayā viññāṇaṃ: with volitional activities as condition, consciousness
viññāṇapaccayā nāmarūpaṃ: with consciousness as condition, name-and-form
nāmarūpapaccayā saḷāyatanaṃ: with name-and-form as condition, the six sense bases
saḷāyatanapaccayā phasso: with the six sense bases as condition, contact
phassapaccayā vedanā: with contact as condition, feeling
vedanāpaccayā taṇhā: with feeling as condition, craving
taṇhāpaccayā upādānaṃ: with craving as condition, clinging
upādānapaccayā bhavo: with clinging as condition, existence
bhavapaccayā jāti: with existence as condition, birth
jātipaccayā jarāmaraṇaṃ: with birth as condition, old-age-and-death

5.1 *Cattāro satipaṭṭhānā*: the four establishments of mindfulness
kāye kāyānupassī: contemplating the body in the body
vedanāsu vedanānupassī: contemplating feelings in feelings
citte cittānupassī: contemplating the mind in the mind
dhammesu dhammānupassī: contemplating phenomena in phenomena

5.2 *Satta bojjhaṅgā*: the seven factors of enlightenment
satisambojjhaṅga: the enlightenment factor of mindfulness
dhammavicayasambojjhaṅga: the enlightenment factor of discrimination of qualities
viriyasambojjhaṅga: the enlightenment factor of energy
pītisambojjhaṅga: the enlightenment factor of rapture
passaddhisambojjhaṅga: the enlightenment factor of tranquility
samādhisambojjhaṅga: the enlightenment factor of concentration
upekkhāsambojjhaṅga: the enlightenment factor of equanimity

5.3 *Ariya aṭṭhaṅgika magga*: the noble eightfold path
sammādiṭṭhi: right view
sammāsaṅkappa: right intention
sammāvācā: right speech
sammākammanta: right action
sammā-ājīva: right livelihood
sammāvāyāma: right effort
sammāsati: right mindfulness
sammāsamādhi: right concentration

6. *Asaṅkhata*: the unconditioned
rāgakkhaya: the destruction of lust
dosakkhaya: the destruction of hatred
mohakkhaya: the destruction of delusion

Notes

1. On the case for the authenticity of these texts, see Sujato and Brahmali 2014.
2. For examples of this systematic way of teaching, see DN 3 (I 110), DN 5 (I 148), MN 56 (I 380), and MN 91 (II 144).
3. The sutta is SN 56:11, at V 420–24.
4. The five aggregates are the subject of the following chapter in this book.
5. Nyanatiloka 1981, 14–15.
6. Nyanatiloka 1981, 14.
7. This account is at MN I 23, MN I 117, MN I 249, AN IV 178–79, and Vin III 5. The word *āsava* is derived from the verb *savati*, meaning "to flow." It is uncertain whether the direction of the flow is intended to be inward or outward. Some translators have rendered *āsava* as "outflow," others as "canker," "taint," "intoxicant," and "pollutant." The three *āsavas* are sensual craving, craving for existence, and ignorance.
8. On the four stages, see Bodhi 2005, 373–81.
9. *Yogo karaṇīyo*. Spk III 293: "Since a monk who is concentrated understands the four noble truths, therefore, when you have gained concentration, an exertion should be made for the purpose of correctly understanding the four noble truths."
10. *Kāmataṇhā, bhavataṇhā, vibhavataṇhā*. Strangely, the suttas themselves do not offer explicit definitions of these three kinds of craving. Vibh 365 (§916), an Abhidhamma text, offers several definitions. It first explains *bhavataṇhā* as "lust and attachment connected with the view of existence"—that is, the eternalist view; *vibhavataṇhā* as "lust and attachment connected with the annihilationist view"; and *kāmataṇhā* as the remaining types of craving. It then offers an alternative. *Kāmataṇhā* is the lust and attachment connected with the sensual realm; *bhavataṇhā* is the lust and attachment connected with the form and formless realms; and *vibhavataṇhā* is the lust and attachment connected with the annihilationist

view. I would propose a simpler explanation: *kāmataṇhā* is craving for sensual pleasures; *bhavataṇhā* is craving for continued existence; and *vibhavataṇhā* is craving for personal annihilation.

11. The sutta is also included in the *Mahāparinibbāna Sutta* (DN 16, at II 90–91).
12. The verbal forms used are *sandhāvitaṃ saṃsaritaṃ*. The latter is the past participle of *saṃsarati*, from which the noun *saṃsāra* is derived.
13. "Conduit to existence" renders *bhavanetti*. Sv II 543 comments: "The rope of craving capable of leading from existence to existence has been thoroughly destroyed, cut off, made incapable of occurring" (*bhavato bhavaṃ nayanasamatthā taṇhārajju suṭṭhu hatā chinnā appavattikatā*).
14. On the influxes (*āsava*), see p. 20.
15. *Tathāni avitathāni anaññathāni*. The three terms, as nouns, are used in relation to dependent origination; see **4.5**.
16. This passage implicitly contains a condensed statement of the sequence of dependent origination. Not seeing the four noble truths is ignorance; delighting in volitional activities that lead to birth, etc., is craving. Generating these volitional activities themselves is the second factor in the stock formula. And falling down the precipice of birth, etc., is birth and old-age-and-death.
17. *Ariyasāvakassa diṭṭhisampannassa puggalassa abhisametāvino*: This refers to a person at the minimum level of stream-enterer. The most sluggish stream-enterer has a maximum of seven more lives, but more acute stream-enterers and those at higher levels of attainment have still fewer lives remaining.
18. For the sutta definitions of the four elements, see MN I 185–89, MN I 421–22, MN III 240–41, and Vibh 82–84 (§§172–76). For the commentarial explanation, see Vism 363–64.
19. According to the Abhidhamma, the tactile object consists of three of the primary elements themselves: the earth element, the fire element, and the air element.
20. At AN III 415: *Cetanāhaṃ, bhikkhave, kammaṃ vadāmi. Cetayitvā kammaṃ karoti kāyena vācāya manasā.*
21. This statement, however, is blurred by SN 22:79 (at III 87), which defines *saññā* as the perception of different colors and *viññāṇa* as the knowing of different flavors. Certainly *saññā* is also involved in the cognition of flavors and *viññāṇa* in the cognition of colors.
22. Spk II 264 explains that this is "the ultimate full understanding, the overcoming" (*accantapariññaṃ, samatikkamanti attho*).
23. *Pañcavaggiyā bhikkhū*. These are the five monks to whom the

Buddha spoke the first discourse, the *Dhammacakkappavattana Sutta*. This sutta, it is said, was spoken a week later.

24. *Labbhetha ca rūpe: 'Evaṃ me rūpaṃ hotu, evaṃ me rūpaṃ mā ahosī'ti.* The sentence implies that if the aggregates were the self, one would be able to exercise absolute control over them, to bend them to one's will.
25. *Anupādāya āsavehi cittāni vimucciṃsu.* This means they attained arahantship.
26. Spk II 215, commenting on the same statement at SN 18:21, explains *saviññāṇake kāye bahiddhā ca sabbanimittesu* as "one's own sentient body and the sentient bodies of others, along with material form disconnected from consciousness. Or, alternatively, by the former is meant the sentient bodies of oneself and others, and by the latter external material form not connected with sense faculties." Regarding *ahaṅkāramamaṅkāramānānusayā*, the commentary identifies "I-making" with views [of self], "mine-making" with craving, and the last as tendencies to conceit. But the compound is so constructed that *anusaya* might also be connected with all three terms, as tendencies toward "I-making," "mine-making," and "conceit."
27. Spk II 288 explains that the expression "for the most part" (*yebhuyyena*) makes exception of those devas who are noble disciples. For devas who are arahants, no fear at all arises. For the other devas, the "knowledge of fearfulness" arises at the time of strong insight.
28. *Sakkāyapariyāpannā. Sakkāya*, "the personal-assemblage," is the assemblage of the five aggregates subject to clinging.
29. This sutta also occurs as MN 109. The "fifteenth" (*pannarasa*) is the fifteenth day of the fortnight, the full-moon night.
30. *Ime kho, bhikkhu, pañcupādānakkhandhā chandamūlakā.* Spk II 307 identifies *chanda* here with craving (*taṇhā*). The statement can be interpreted to mean that the present assemblage of five aggregates has arisen on account of the craving from the prior life that brought them into being in this life.
31. Spk II 307 explains that it is said "clinging itself is not [the same as] those five clinging-aggregates" because the five aggregates are not simply desire-and-lust. But it is said "there is no clinging apart from the five clinging-aggregates" because there is no clinging separate from the aggregates, without occurring along with them or taking them as its object.
32. Spk II 321 explains at length how form (i.e., the body) is like a lump of foam (*pheṇapiṇḍa*). To give merely the highlights: As a lump of foam lacks any substance (*sāra*), so form lacks any substance that is permanent, stable, or a self; as the lump of foam is full of fissures and the abode of many creatures, so too

form; as the lump of foam breaks up, so does form, which is pulverized in the mouth of Death.

33. Spk II 322: A bubble (*bubbuḷa*) is feeble and cannot be grasped, for it breaks up as soon as it is seized; so too feeling is feeble and cannot be grasped as permanent and stable. As a bubble arises and ceases and does not last long, so too millions of feelings arise and cease in the time of a finger snap. As a bubble depends on conditions, so too feeling depends on a sense base, an object, the defilements, and contact.
34. Spk II 322: Perception is like a mirage (*marīci*) in the sense that it is insubstantial, for one cannot grasp a mirage [of water] to drink or bathe or fill a pitcher. As a mirage deceives the multitude, so does perception, which entices people with the idea that the object is beautiful, pleasurable, and permanent.
35. Spk II 323: As a plantain trunk (*kadalikkhandha*) is an assemblage of many sheaths, each with its own characteristic, so the aggregate of volitional activities is an assemblage of many mental factors, such as contact, volition, etc., each with its own characteristic.
36. Spk II 323: Consciousness is like a magical illusion (*māyā*) in the sense that it is insubstantial and cannot be grasped. Consciousness is even more transient and fleeting than a magical illusion. For it gives the impression that a person comes and goes, stands and sits, with the same mind, but the mind is different in each of these activities. Consciousness deceives the multitude like a magical illusion.
37. *Ādiccabandhu*: an epithet of the Buddha.
38. Vibh 71 (§161): *Chabbidhena manāyatanaṃ: cakkhuviññāṇaṃ, sotaviññāṇaṃ, ghānaviññāṇaṃ, jivhāviññāṇaṃ, kāyaviññāṇaṃ, manoviññāṇaṃ.*
39. The formula is found, among many other places, at DN I 70, MN I 180–81, SN IV 104, and AN II 210.
40. AN 3:16 (at I 113–14).
41. *Na nimittaggāhī hoti nānubyañjanaggāhī.*
42. The sutta is also at Vin I 34–35. The thousand monks, according to this account, were former matted-hair ascetics (*jaṭila*) who maintained the sacred fire. Hence a discourse on the theme of "burning" suited their disposition.
43. Sakka is the ruler of the devas in the Tāvatiṃsa Heaven.
44. Here, and throughout this book, to replicate the style of the Pāli, I render *jarāmaraṇaṃ* (a copula compound of the singular type) as a hyphenated singular.
45. *Imasmiṃ sati idaṃ hoti, imass'uppādā idaṃ uppajjati; imasmiṃ asati idaṃ na hoti, imassa nirodhā idaṃ nirujjhati.*

46. In fact, AN 3:61 (at I 177) expressly explains the second and third noble truths with the formula for dependent origination respectively in the orders of arising and cessation.
47. See for example the definitions of these terms at Vibh 145 (§249).
48. This compound is often rendered "mentality-materiality," which may be doctrinally more accurate, but to connect the expression with its earlier usage in Indian thought, I render it literally as "name-and-form." For Vedic philosophy, *nāmarūpa* is the manifestation of the unitary reality, *brahman*, in the mode of multiplicity, apprehended by the senses as diversified appearances or forms, and by thought as diversified names or concepts. The Buddha adopted this expression and invested it with a meaning consonant with his own system, where it represents the physical and cognitive sides of sentient existence.
49. The three-life interpretation of dependent origination, it should be stressed, was by no means peculiar to the Theravāda school, but was shared, with minor differences in details, by the other schools of Early Buddhism that have left records of their doctrinal systems.
50. On this mode of treatment, see Vism 579–81 (Ñāṇamoli 2010, 601–3); Bodhi 1993, 299–300. The method of explanation originates with the Paṭisambhidāmagga, an exegetical work included in the Sutta Piṭaka. It is quoted in the above passage of Vism.
51. See Vism 58; Bodhi (1993), 300–301.
52. These are the three realms of existence in Buddhist cosmology. For details, see Bodhi 1993, 189–93.
53. Though I render *nāma* as name, this should not be taken too literally. *Nāma* is the assemblage of mental factors involved in cognition: feeling, perception, volition, contact, and attention. These are called "name" because they contribute to the process of cognition by which objects are conceptualized and subsumed under verbal designations.
54. The Pāli terms are *kāyasaṅkhāra, vacīsaṅkhāra*, and *cittasaṅkhāra*. Vibh 135 (§226) defines them as three kinds of volition thus: *kāyasañcetanā kāyasaṅkhāro, vacīsañcetanā vacīsaṅkhāro, manosañcetanā cittasaṅkhāro*. These three *saṅkhārā* should not be confused with the threefold set discussed in MN 44 (at I 301) and SN 41:6 (at IV 293). Though the designations are the same, the latter triad is always spoken of in relation to the cessation of perception and feeling and never in connection with dependent origination. They are defined respectively as in-and-out breathing, thought and examination, and perception and feeling.
55. Spk II 21 explains *yoniso manasikāra* as "attention that is

methodical, attention that is on track" (*upāyamanasikārena pathamanasikārena*).

56. Spk II 23 explains nutriment as a condition: "for conditions bring along their own fruit, thus they are called nutriments" (*paccayā hi āharanti attano phalaṃ, tasmā āhārāti vuccanti*). What is evidently intended here are *strong* conditions: material food for the body, contact for feeling, mental volition for renewed existence in the three realms, and consciousness for name-and-form.
57. The Buddha rejects his question because it presupposes the existence of a self that lies behind consciousness. The same presupposition of a self underlies his following questions.
58. It would be misleading to translate the two terms, *atthitā* and *natthitā*, simply as "existence" and "nonexistence" and then to maintain (as is sometimes done) that the Buddha rejects all ontological notions as inherently invalid. The Buddha's statements at **2.14**, for example, show that he makes pronouncements about what exists and what does not exist when such pronouncements are called for. In the present passage *atthitā* and *natthitā* are abstract nouns formed by adding the abstract suffix *-tā* to the verbs *atthi* and *natthi*. It is the *metaphysical assumptions* implicit in such abstractions that are at fault, not the ascriptions of existence and non-existence themselves.
59. For the Buddha's teaching on the origin and passing away of the world, see SN 12:44, not included here.
60. *Dhammaṭṭhitatā dhammaniyāmatā idappaccayatā*. In the first two compounds, it is hard to determine on the basis of the text itself whether *dhamma* is a singular signifying "the Dhamma," that is, the law of conditionality governing phenomena, or a plural, *dhammā*, signifying the phenomena governed by the law. Spk II 40 takes the two expressions to refer to the condition (*paccaya*), "for it is through the condition that the conditionally arisen phenomena persist and it is the condition that governs phenomena."
61. *Iti kho, bhikkhave, yā tatra tathatā avitathatā anaññathatā idappaccayatā, ayaṃ vuccati, bhikkhave, paṭiccasamuppādo*. See **1.7**, where the corresponding adjectives, *tatha, avitatha, anaññatha*, describe the four noble truths.
62. The Buddha's ten powers and four kinds of self-confidence are at MN 12 (I 69–72).
63. *Jarāmaraṇanirodhasāruppagāminī paṭipadā*. This is an unusual way of describing the practice. Spk II 77 explains that the way is said to be "in conformity with the cessation of old-age-and-death" because it is *similar to* cessation on account of its purity and absence of defilements (*nikkilesatāya parisuddhatāya sadisāva*).

64. The three are: *puññābhisaṅkhāra, apuññābhisaṅkhāra, āneñjābhisaṅkhāra*. Vibh 135 (§226) explains meritorious volitional activity as wholesome volition of the desire sphere and the form sphere, generated by giving, ethical behavior, and mental development (*kusalā cetanā kāmāvacarā rūpāvacarā dānamayā sīlamayā bhāvanāmayā*). Demeritorious volitional activity is unwholesome volition of the desire sphere (*akusalā cetanā kāmāvacarā*). Imperturbable volitional activity is wholesome volition of the formless sphere (*kusalā cetanā arūpāvacarā*). Spk II 78 explains that the karmic consciousness "approaches the meritorious," etc., by being associated with the corresponding ethical quality; the resultant consciousness "approaches the meritorious," etc., by arriving at the result of meritorious activity, etc.
65. On the distinction between the nibbāna element with residue and the nibbāna element without residue, see pp. 159–60. Though the present sutta does not use these expressions, it seems the distinction is implied here.
66. Spk II 78: "A 'feeling limited by the body' (*kāyapariyantikaṃ vedanaṃ*) is a feeling through the five sense doors, which occurs as long as the body continues. A 'feeling limited by life' (*jīvitapariyantikaṃ vedanaṃ*) is a feeling through the mind-door, which occurs as long as life continues."
67. Spk II 81: "This is the end, the termination, of the dukkha of the round of existence, namely, nibbāna."
68. At SN 22:121, the five aggregates are called "things that can be clung to" (*upādāniyā dhammā*). At SN 35:110 the same term is ascribed to the six internal sense bases, and at SN 35:123 to the six external bases—that is, delightful forms, sounds, etc.
69. *Imasmiṃ cātumahābhūtikasmiṃ kāyasmiṃ*. Literally, "in this body composed of the four great elements."
70. *Yañca kho etaṃ, bhikkhave, vuccati cittaṃ itipi, mano itipi, viññāṇaṃ itipi*. Generally, in the suttas these three terms occur in different contexts. *Citta* is the center of a person's inner life, the seat of emotions and volitions, that which is subject to defilement and purification; *mano* is the internal sense base and a door of action; and *viññāṇa* is the awareness that makes possible cognition through the six sense bases. But here they are treated as three designations for the same entity.
71. The line of inquiry described here may be compared with that described at **4.2**. Whereas the former traces the chain of conditions back to volitional activities and ignorance, the present version ends with the interdependence of consciousness and name-and-form.
72. Consciousness can be regarded as dependent on name-and-form insofar as, in human experience, consciousness requires

"form," a physical body equipped with sense faculties, and always arises in association with feeling, perception, volition, contact, and attention, the constituents of "name." Name-and-form is dependent on consciousness insofar as the physical body only functions as a sentient body when inhabited by consciousness, and the factors of the "name" group can only occur in association with consciousness.

73. *Upadhinidānaṃ upadhisamudayaṃ upadhijātikaṃ upadhipabhavaṃ.* Spk II 119 explains *upadhi* here as the five aggregates (*khandha-pañcakaṃ h'ettha upadhīti adhippetaṃ*).
74. The four immeasurables (*appamaññā*), also known as the *brahmavihāras*, are boundless loving-kindness, compassion, altruistic joy, and equanimity (see DN 13, MN 7, MN 40, etc.). The four means of sustaining a relationship (*saṅgahavatthu*) are giving, pleasant speech, beneficial conduct, and equality of treatment (see AN 4:32, AN 9:5, etc.).
75. *Vivekanissitaṃ virāganissitaṃ nirodhanissitaṃ vossaggapariṇāmiṃ.*
76. *Rāgavinayapariyosānaṃ dosavinayapariyosānaṃ mohavinaya-pariyosānaṃ.*
77. On "a path going in one direction" (*ekāyana magga*), see pp. 122–23. Spk III 177 says it is called thus because "it is not a forked path" (*na dvedhāpathabhūto*). It identifies "the method" (*ñāya*) with the noble eightfold path. For my summary of the content of the four establishments of mindfulness, see pp. 120–22.
78. Technically, the trainee (*sekha*) is one who has entered the irreversible path to nibbāna but has not yet reached the goal. It comprises seven classes of noble disciples: those on the four paths—to stream-entry, once-returning, non-returning, and arahantship—and those who have attained the lower three fruits. The arahant, who has attained the fourth fruit, is called *asekha*, "one not in training, one finished with the training."
79. The readings in various editions differ, and none is particularly clear. The text may have been corrupted here, so my rendering is speculative.
80. By entering "the rains" (*vassa*), the Buddha refers to the three-month rains residence, extending roughly from July to October, when monastics stop wandering and remain at a fixed residence.
81. *Anantaraṃ abāhiraṃ.* Spk III 203 explains: "Without making a distinction of inside and outside with respect either to the teaching or to persons. One makes the distinction with respect to the teaching when one thinks, 'I will teach so much to others but this much I won't teach.' One does so with respect to persons when one thinks, 'I'll teach this person but not that one.' The Buddha did not teach in this way. The 'teacher's

closed fist' (*ācariyamuṭṭhi*) is found among outsiders, who reserve certain teachings for their favorite pupils only when they are lying on their deathbed; but the Buddha did not act like this."

82. *Animittaṃ cetosamādhiṃ*. Spk III 204 identifies this with the attainment of fruition (*phalasamāpatti*), the meditative absorption in nibbāna.
83. *Attadīpā viharatha attasaraṇā anaññasaraṇā, dhammadīpā dhammasaraṇā anaññasaraṇā*. *Attadīpā viharatha* is often rendered "be a lamp unto yourselves." The Pāli word *dīpa* is a homonym, which can represent in Sanskrit either *dvīpa*, "island," or *dīpa*, "lamp." Both Sv II 548 (to DN II 100) and Spk III 204 take it in the former sense, stating: "Make yourself a secure island like an island in the great ocean" (*mahāsamuddagatadīpaṃ viya attānaṃ dīpaṃ patiṭṭhaṃ katvā viharatha*).
84. The third of the four fruits of attainment, distinguished by the eradication of the five lower fetters: the view of the personal-assemblage, doubt, wrong grasp of precepts and observances, sensual desire, and ill will. The non-returner no longer takes rebirth in the desire realm but is reborn in one of the higher realms and attains final liberation there.
85. Nāgas are dragon-like beings that dwell in the upper atmosphere and deep in the oceans and the earth, where they guard hidden treasures. They are capable of changing their shape and sometimes appear in human form.
86. On this formula, see p. 124.
87. Spk III 141: "Dark states are 'with counterparts' (*sappaṭibhāgā*) because they yield dark results, and bright states because they yield bright results. . . . Or 'with counterparts' means 'with opposites': the dark states have the bright as their opposites, the bright have the dark as their opposites."
88. Spk III 141: "The element of arousal (*ārambhadhātu*) is the initial phase of energy, the element of endeavour (*nikkamadhātu*) is stronger because one has overcome laziness, while the element of exertion (*parakkamadhātu*) is still stronger because one advances to successively higher levels."
89. *Samathanimittaṃ abyagganimittaṃ*. Spk III 141 takes the two to be synonyms and identifies them with serenity itself as well as with the object of serenity.
90. In stating that the enlightenment factor of mindfulness arises by recollecting the Dhamma taught by the monks, the text connects *sati* (from the verb *sarati*, "to remember") as an act of remembrance with the verb *anussarati*, "to recollect." Though overshadowed by *sati*'s more technical sense of awareness of the present, this nuance is still occasionally preserved in Pāli. The

three phrases used to describe the cultivation of each enlightenment factor can be understood to depict three successive stages of development: initial arousal, maturation, and culmination.

91. By "final knowledge" (*aññā*), the attainment of arahantship is indicated, achieved either in the course of life or on the verge of death.
92. These five expressions indicate five modes of attaining the stage of non-returner (*anāgāmī*). Different interpretations of these terms have been proposed. I take the "attainer of nibbāna in the interval" (*antarāparinibbāyī*) to be one who attains full liberation in the intermediate state between death and rebirth, and the "attainer of nibbāna upon landing" (*upahaccaparinibbāyī*) to be one who attains liberation soon after taking rebirth in the form realm. On the lower fetters, see note 84.
93. This one, the *uddhaṃsota akaniṭṭhagāmī*, takes rebirth in successive pure abodes, completes the full lifespan in each, and finally attains arahantship in the Akaniṭṭha realm, the highest pure abode. The pure abodes (*suddhāvāsa*) are five planes in the form realm into which only non-returners can be reborn.
94. *Kalyāṇamittatā kalyāṇasahāyatā kalyāṇasampavaṅkatā*. The three are near synonyms.
95. Earlier translators have misunderstood the grammatical form of *kalyāṇamitto bhikkhu*, taking it to mean either "a monk who is a good friend" or "a monk who is a friend of the good." As an independent substantive, *kalyāṇamitta* means a good friend, but when used in apposition to *bhikkhu*, *kalyāṇamitta* becomes an adjectival compound (*bahubbīhi*), so that the expression means "a monk *who has* a good friend."
96. All editions of SN read here *abrahmacariyā veramaṇī*, "abstinence from impure [sexual] activity," but elsewhere the reading for this facet of right action is *kāmesu micchācārā veramaṇī*, "abstinence from sexual misconduct." The former is found in the precept observed by monastics, the latter in the precept undertaken by the laity. The SN reading may be a scribal error. I have therefore translated on the assumption that the correct reading should be *kāmesu micchācārā veramaṇī*.

Bibliography

Bodhi, Bhikkhu. 1993. *A Comprehensive Manual of Abhidhamma: The Philosophical Psychology of Buddhism*. Kandy, Sri Lanka: Buddhist Publication Society.

———. 2000. *The Connected Discourses of the Buddha: A Translation of the Saṃyutta Nikāya*. Boston: Wisdom Publications.

———. 2005. *In the Buddha's Words: An Anthology of Discourses from the Pali Canon*. Boston: Wisdom Publications.

———. 2020. *Reading the Buddha's Discourses in Pāli: A Practical Guide to the Language of the Ancient Buddhist Canon*. Somerville, MA: Wisdom Publications.

Ñāṇamoli, Bhikkhu, trans. 2010. *The Path of Purification (Visuddhimagga)*. 4th ed. Kandy, Sri Lanka: Buddhist Publication Society.

Nyanatiloka Mahāthera. 1981. *The Word of the Buddha: An Outline of the Teachings of the Buddha in the Words of the Pāli Canon*. 16th ed. Kandy, Sri Lanka: Buddhist Publication Society.

Sujato, Bhikkhu, and Ajahn Brahmali. 2014. *The Authenticity of the Early Buddhist Texts*. https://buddhistuniversity.net/content/booklets/authenticity_sujato-brahmali.

About the Author

Ven. Bhikkhu Bodhi is an American Buddhist monk from New York City, born in 1944. He obtained a BA in philosophy from Brooklyn College and a PhD in philosophy from Claremont Graduate School. After completing his university studies he traveled to Sri Lanka, where he received novice ordination in 1972 and full ordination in 1973, both under the leading Sri Lankan scholar-monk Ven. Balangoda Ānanda Maitreya Mahānāyaka Thera (1896–1998). From 1984 to 2002 he was the editor for the Buddhist Publication Society in Kandy, where he lived for ten years with the senior German monk Ven. Nyanaponika Mahāthera (1901–94) at the Forest Hermitage. He returned to the United States in 2002. He currently lives and teaches at Chuang Yen Monastery in Carmel, New York. Ven. Bodhi has many important publications to his credit, either as author, translator, or editor. These include *The Middle Length Discourses of the Buddha* (Majjhima Nikāya, 1995), *The Connected Discourses of the Buddha* (Saṃyutta Nikāya, 2000), *The Numerical Discourses of the Buddha* (Aṅguttara Nikāya, 2012), and *The Suttanipāta* (2017). In 2008, together with several of his students, Ven. Bodhi founded Buddhist Global Relief, a nonprofit supporting hunger relief, sustainable agriculture, and education in countries suffering from chronic poverty and malnutrition.

What to Read Next from Wisdom Publications

Reading the Buddha's Discourses in Pāli
A Practical Guide to the Language of the Ancient Buddhist Canon
Texts selected, translated, and explained by Bhikkhu Bodhi

"Every student of Pāli will welcome Bhikkhu Bodhi's *Reading the Buddha's Discourses in Pāli.*"—Charles Hallisey, author of *Therigatha: Poems of the First Buddhist Women*

The Connected Discourses of the Buddha
A Translation of the Saṃyutta Nikāya
Bhikkhu Bodhi

"To hold a copy of *The Connected Discourses of the Buddha* is like holding treasure in your hands."—*Eastern Horizon*

In the Buddha's Words
An Anthology of Discourses from the Pāli Canon
Bhikkhu Bodhi

"It will rapidly become the sourcebook of choice for both neophyte and serious students alike."—*Buddhadharma*

The Middle Length Discourses of the Buddha
A Translation of the Majjhima Nikāya
Bhikkhu Ñāṇamoli and Bhikkhu Bodhi

"As close as we'll get to the original teachings and account of the life of the Buddha."—*Tricycle*

About Wisdom Publications

Wisdom Publications is the leading publisher of classic and contemporary Buddhist books and practical works on mindfulness. To learn more about us or to explore our other books, please visit our website at wisdomexperience.org or contact us at the address below.

Wisdom Publications
132 Perry Street
New York, NY 10014 USA

We are a 501(c)(3) organization, and donations in support of our mission are tax deductible.

Wisdom Publications is affiliated with the Foundation for the Preservation of the Mahayana Tradition (FPMT).